The Best Chronicles
of Rubem Alves

Other Books in New London Librarium's
Brazil Series

Eternal Tender Returns: Essays by Rubem Alves

Miss Dollar: Stories by Machado de Assis

Ex Cathedra: Stories by Machado de Assis

Religions in Rio

Quilombo dos Palmares:
Brazil's Lost Nation of Fugitive Slaves

Law of the Jungle: Environmental Anarchy and
the Tenharim People of Amazonia

Journey on the Estrada Real:
Encounters in the Mountains of Brazil

Promised Land: A Nun's Struggle against Landlessness,
Lawlessness, Slavery, Injustice, Corruption, and
Environmental Devastation in Amazonia

THE BEST CHRONICLES
OF RUBEM ALVES

with a Foreword by
Raquel Alves

translated by
Glenn Alan Cheney

New London Librarium

The Best Chronicles of Rubem Alves
by Rubem Alves
Foreword by Raquel Alves
Introduction by Ana Lessa-Schmidt
Translated by Glenn Alan Cheney

Original title: *As Melhores Crônicas de Rubem Alves*,
published in Campinas, S.P., Brazil, by Editora Papyrus.

Published by
New London Librarium
P.O. Box 284
Hanover, CT 06350
NLLibrarium.com

ISBNs
Hardcover: 978-0-9982730-5-9
Paperback: 978-0-9966747-8-2
eBook: 978-0-9966747-9-9

PRINTED IN THE UNITED STATES

Contents

$\mathcal{F}$oreword

$\mathcal{I}n$ his article "An Anthropophagous Ritual," Rubem Alves wrote:

> Anthropophagy is the eating of human flesh—cannibalism, something savage. But so-called savages don't think so. A tribe of Brazilian Indians who practiced anthropophagy justified it thus: "You who call yourselves civilized don't love your dead. You make deep holes and bury them to be eaten by worms. We, on the other hand, love our dead. We don't want them to be dead. But they are dead! There is only one way to keep them alive: if we eat them. If we eat them, their flesh and blood continue to live in our own bodies.
>
> Anthropophagy isn't done for nutritional reasons. It isn't a barbecue. It's a magical ceremony. It is believed that, by eating the dead,

their virtues are incorporated into those who eat them. Psychoanalysts agree. They believe that our personality is formed by successive anthropophagous meals at which we devour a piece of one person, a piece of another. Of course, they don't use the word "anthropophagy." They use the word "introjection," which means "to put inside." But "to put inside" is, precisely, to eat.

The eucharist is a poetic ritual of anthropophagy. "This bread is my body; eat of it. This wine is my blood: drink of it."

The Minas Gerais writer Murilo Mendes, in his book *A hora do Serrote [The Time of the Saw]* says something more or less like this: "In the time when I wasn't an anthropophagus—in the time when I wasn't devouring books—for aren't books made of the flesh and blood of those who wrote them?"

Because that's what I wish: to be eaten.

Rubem Alves had an astonishing outlook on life. Its mysteries and beauties, which appeared day after day, from the magnificent sunsets to the minute details drawn on the wings of butterflies, did not pass unnoticed before his eyes. It was always magic, and the world was a source of mysteries that, if viewed with sensibility, awaken within us the pleasure of life. Readers who devour the author through his writings transform their view. And they see the world through the eyes of Rubem Alves. *The Best Chronicles of Rubem Alves* awakens us to a world of sensible intelligence, speaking to us about our quotidian life, our loves and the scenes of life. My wish is that Rubem Alves be anthropophagically devoured so that his essence, his way of thinking, seeing and loving become part of the reader's body.

RAQUEL ALVES
CAMPINAS, SP - BRAZIL

x

Introduction

I "found" Rubem Alves as a teenager, exactly at that phase that we all develop a need to define ourselves. His intimations of wisdom helped me more than most of the people around me in the 'real' world, the world outside his words. Since then, his thoughts have resonated in my life. His 'lessons' became part of who I am and the way I think, act, and react towards life. In his own words: "Books eaten with pleasure are books to be ruminated for life. Ruminated books are not forgotten books."

If I were asked: "Which Rubem Alves do you like best? The theologian? The teacher? The intellectual? The poet? The psychoanalyst? The author of children's books? The political activist?," I would certainly answer: "I prefer them all." In each of these men there are lessons to be drawn. So, decades after I first met him in his words, it's an honor for me to write a humble introduction to The Best Chronicles of Rubem Alves. It's an insightful translation of select essays by a word whisperer who tames ideas. As he renders them in simple words, we feel their power without restrictions or fears. We can share his poetic and fatherly sense of the world.

If this were another edition in Portuguese, Rubem Alves wouldn't even need to be introduced. Most Brazilians would have heard of this man and respect him as an educator, philosopher, even, in my particular case, a kind of guru. Maybe he was actually the one who inspired the title of Mario Quintana's *O Aprendiz de Feiticeiro (The Sorcerer's Apprentice)* (1950), as Rubem Alves never ceased to enchant those who read him.

Bullied as a child because of his strong accent from Minas Gerais, he rose above those who ridiculed him. He found solace and refuge in religion, becoming a poet, writer, and pedagogue. and Brazilians found solace in his theosophical thoughts. "I thought religion wasn't to secure heaven after death," he wrote, "but to make this world better, while we are alive."

With the birth of his youngest daughter he learned that he could write for children. In 1963 he went to study in New York. On his return in 1964, a month after the military coup d'état which would oppress the country for over 20 years, the same church that had been his refuge and inspiration now denounced him as subversive. He had to flee back to the U.S. with his family, where he went to study at Princeton Theological Seminary. There he wrote his Ph.D.s thesis *Towards a Theology of Liberation*, which was published in 1969 as *A Theology of Human Hope*. The document is considered by many as the real foundation for Liberation Theology. In 1968, one of the toughest years of the dictatorship, he returned to Brazil and became a philosophy professor. He stayed with that profession until his last breath. Teaching was a philosophy for life, and death. In his work he touches upon a wide variety of subjects relating to human interaction and struggles, both on the positive and negative sides of the sphere. In his own words: "Inside me lives a clown and a poet: laughter and beauty... If I weren't a writer, I think I would be a gardener. In heaven, God didn't build altars and cathedrals. He planted a garden. God is a gardener. That's why planting gardens is the highest form of spirituality. I believe, as a poet and clown, that the heavenly fruit was a persimmon..."

When I asked Glenn Cheney, who knows the writer's work through his personal and professional links with Brazil, about the experience of translating someone like Rubem Alves, he told me that it was a great pleasure,

> because his style of writing is very modern. Short sentences. Simple words. This fact is quite significant because he uses simple words to explain

matters that seem, on the surface, to be simple—
the beauty of trees, the goodness of friends, the
role of rituals, the warmth of candle light, the
beauty of human life. But at the same time, he
is writing of the depth behind simple things. He
may be writing about the pleasures of sex, the
meaning of names, the value of uselessness, but
one needn't read far before encountering the word
soul. I think it's in every essay.

That is true. The word "soul" appears some 31 times
in this book. But it's also true that the word life appears 32
times, and death 27 times. But love is the great champion
in the marathon of the word count in this collection. It
appears no fewer than 240 times.

And love is what we feel in our souls when we read
him. Love for our self, for our neighbour, for our past,
present and future. Love written in the heart. According
to Alves, "That which is written in the heart does not need
agendas because we don't forget it. Whatever the memory
loves remains forever."

The poet confessed that he was not afraid of dying.
He felt sadness about leaving the world that he loved so
much. In 2014, he handed his sadness to readers, followers,
and lovers of words and wisdom.

Fortunately his work lives on through his thoughts
and lessons, in his more than 120 publications. Most of

those works have yet to be translated and spread around the globe. High praises should be given to New London Librarium for its Brazilian Series of books. And a nod of thanks is due Glenn Alan Cheney, who understands the worth of Rubem Alves's work reaching out to wider readership. Brazil's Fundação Biblioteca Nacional also deserves credit for sponsoring such an important translation of essays by one of the most popular and respected writers in Brazil.

Praises are given to yet another book being born into this world today, because according to Rubem Alves:

> Books need to be within reach of hands. Everywhere. In the living room, bathroom, kitchen, bedroom. A small bookshelf near the toilet is very useful for quickly read books. Art books, for example! It's important that children and young adults learn that books are worlds through which we make delightful excursions. Of course! For this, there must be guides.

I invite readers to allow this master to guide them into the magical world of words which, if used with care and love in any language, make us more human and more a part of humanity.

ANA LESSA-SCHMIDT, PH.D.
BARCELONA

Walking in the Morning

For the past two weeks I've been starting my days
by committing theft. I don't know how to avoid this
sin, and, to tell the truth, I don't want to avoid it. The guilt
is from a mulberry tree. Disobeying the commandment
of the wall that fences it in, it thrusts its branches over
the sidewalk. Not satisfied, it loads them with fat, black,
appetizing, tempting mulberries [in Portuguese, *amoras*]
within reach of my hand. It seems that the fruits are, by
vocation, invitations to theft: changing the order of a single
letter is enough. I think that the case of the mulberry tree
proves this linguistic thesis: Everything depends on a name.
Because *amora* is a word which, if repeated several times,
amoramoramoramora turns into *amor*—love. And isn't that
what love is?—a desire to eat, a desire to be eaten. The
wall, much like a commandment, says it is prohibited. But

17

love is not contained. Cross-dressed as a mulberry, it jumps the fence. Thus it was in Paradise...

The few strollers passing by at that hour of the morning were perhaps surprised to see a man with white hair picking prohibited mulberries. But if they pay attention, they will see that the person who's there isn't a man of nearly seventy years. It's a boy. And since it was the son of God himself who said to enter the Kingdom of Heaven you need to return to childhood, I pick and eat mulberries with redoubled conviction. And just so no doubts remain about the theological inspiration of my deed, as I chew and the purple juice stains my fingers and mouth, I repeat the sacred words: "Eat and drink, this is my blood..." Ah! The divine mulberry, sacramental gift of grace! My day begins this way, stealing the magic fruit that works the miracle of everyone who dreams of returning to childhood.

Body and soul reinvigorated by this divine manna fallen from the skies, I continue along my morning walk. I walk no more than fifty steps and I'm under a long alameda of pines. On them there's no fruit for me to steal since they don't produce anything that can be eaten. Pines aren't for the mouth. They are gifts for the eyes. It's still early. The sun, just risen, illuminates their green needles, which shine like crystals. I am reminded of Le Corbusier, who said, "The essential joys are sun, space, and green." But the pines know more than the architect, and the joys of light feed the joys of smell. I breathe deeply and smell the aroma of resin.

If they ask me what I think, I answer with a line from the Tao: "The sound of water says what I think." I think the mulberries, I think the pine, I think the light of the sun, I think the smell of resin.

It's the season of *sibipiruna* tree blossoms. Green and yellow, they grow on both sides of the street where I walk, transforming it into a long, shady tunnel. During the night, their flowers fell, covering the sidewalk, turning it into a golden carpet. I step off the sidewalk and walk on the asphalt so to not tread on them. I am reminded of the mysterious voice that spoke to Moses from inside the burning bush: "Put off thy shoes from off thy feet, for the place whereon thou standest is holy ground."

To contemplate this spectacle, you have to get up early because soon the housewives and their brooms will take care of restoring the concrete to its cold cleanliness. This hurts me, and with the pain comes a thought. I ask myself about the perverse education that makes people become blind to the generous beauty of trees, treating their blossoms as if they were dirt. But the *sibipirunas*, indifferent to the blindness of humans and broom, will repeat the miracle during the night. Tomorrow the sidewalks will again be covered in gold.

I walk a bit more and come to the grove called the

Bosque dos Alemães. It awaits me with another delight, the delight of the ears. An infinitude of birdsong mixes with the sound of leaves blown by the breeze. I am not alone. Many other people dedicated to the exercise of morning walks and runs keep me company. They are there in fear of dying before their time. It's necessary to exercise the heart. But it seems that's all they're exercising. But no matter how hard I try, I can't manage to see in their faces signs that they are also exercising the delight of their eyes, noses, and ears. They run and walk with eyes fixed on the ground, serious and focused, compelled by medical necessities. And for that reason they do not know how to see and hear, can't handle a stirring love affair unrolling before them. I'd been sensing romance for a while when I heard sighs came from on high. Up there, far from indiscreet eyes, a giant eucalyptus and a cork tree embrace. Their intertwined branches manifest the passion of lovers. I think they're making love because as the wind makes their bark rub against each other, they moan with pleasure…and pain.

I walk all morning. For medical reasons, it's true. But, even if they didn't exist, I'd walk the same way, with the light and joyful thoughts that nature makes me think. Nature is a good psychoanalyst, charging nothing for the dreams of love she makes us dream.

How Goodness Happens

"If they asked you who it was that wanted to teach springtime to the sand and ice..." That is how Cecília Meireles begins one of her poems. To teach springtime to the sand and ice is difficult. Ice and sand know nothing of spring. So I would like to know how to teach solidarity to someone who knows nothing about it. The world would be better off. But how to teach it?

Is it possible to teach the beauty of a Mozart sonata to the deaf? How, if they can't hear? And am I capable of teaching the beauty of the paintings of Monet to the blind? What good would pedagogy be to communicate colors and shapes to someone who can't see? There are things that cannot be taught. There are things that are beyond words. Scientists, philosophers, and professors are people who dedicate themselves to teaching things that can be taught. Things that can be taught are things that can be spoken.

In solidarity, many things can be spoken. For example: I think it is possible to develop a psychology of solidarity. I think it is also possible to develop a sociology of solidarity. And, philosophically, an ethic of solidarity. But scientists and philosophers with expertise in solidarity do not teach solidarity. In the same way, music and art critics do not teach people the beauty of music and art.

Words that teach are cages for birds that can be caged. Experts, all of them, are caged birds. But solidarity is a bird that cannot be caged. It cannot be spoken. Solidarity belongs to a class of birds that only exist in flight. These birds, caged, die.

Beauty is one of these birds. Beauty is beyond words. Walt Whitman was aware of this when he said: "Sermons and logic never convince. The damp of the night drives deeper into my soul." He knew the limits of his own words. And Fernando Pessoa knew that that which the poet wants to communicate is not found in the words he uses; rather, it appears in the empty spaces that open among them. In this empty space a song can be heard. But this song—where does it come from if it wasn't the poet that played it?

It is not possible to take a test on beauty because it is not knowledge. Nor is it possible to order emotion in the face of beauty. Only acts can be ordered. "Parade...march!" the sergeant orders. The recruits obey. They march. The act follows the order. But feelings cannot be ordered. I can't order someone to sense the beauty that I am sensing.

What can be taught are things that reside in the outside world: astronomy, physics, chemistry grammar, anatomy, numbers, letters, words.

But there are things that are not on the outside. Things that reside inside the body. They are buried in the flesh as if they were seeds in waiting...

Yes, yes! Imagine this: the body as a big garden! In it we find a wide variety of seeds, sleeping in a state of latency—remember the story of Sleeping Beauty! They can awaken, sprout. But they can also not sprout. It all depends. Seeds don't sprout if there's a stone over them. And it can also happen that, after sprouting, they get pulled up. In fact, many plants need to be pulled up before they grow. In gardens there are such pests: crab grass, weeds...

One of these seeds is "solidarity." Solidarity isn't an entity in the world outside, on the side of the stars, stones, merchandise, money, contracts. If it were an entity on the outside, it could be taught and produced. Solidarity is an entity of the inner world. Solidarity is neither taught nor ordered nor produced. Solidarity has to sprout and grow like a seed.

23

Look at the lowering *ipê* tree! It was born of a seed. After growing, no technique is necessary, no stimulus, no tricks to get it to blossom. Angeus Silesius, ancient mystic, has a verse that says, "The rose is without reason, blooming because it blooms." The *ipê* blooms because it blooms. Its blossom is simply a natural overflowing of its truth.

Solidarity is like the *ipê*: it is born and blooms. But not in obedience to ethical or religious commandments. It cannot be ordered: "Be in solidarity!" Solidarity happens like a simple overflowing: springs overflow... just the way a poem is an overflowing soul of a poet, music an overflowing of the soul of the composer...

I've already said that solidarity is a feeling. It's the feeling that makes us human. It's a strange feeling that bothers our own feelings. Solidarity makes me feel feelings that aren't mine, that are someone else's. It happens like this: I see a child selling candy at a stoplight. She asks me to buy a pack of her candy. The child and I—two bodies separate and distinct. But, when I see her, I tremble. Something inside makes me imagine what she is feeling. And then, by inexplicable magic, this imagined feeling settles in next to my own feelings. In fact it unsettles my feelings, since I had come there, in my car, with light and happy feelings, and now this new feeling sets itself in the place of them. What I feel isn't my feelings. It's the lightness and happiness that made me sing. Now, it's the feelings of the child that are in me. My body undergoes a transformation. It is no longer limited by the skin that covers it. It expands. It's now connected to another body that becomes part of it itself. This doesn't happen by rational decision or by religious

24

conviction or by ethical commandment. It is the natural way of being of my own body, driven by solidarity. I think this is the meaning of Jesus' dictum that we have to love our neighbor as we love ourselves. Solidarity is the visible form of love. By the magic of the feeling of solidarity, my body becomes the home of another. That's how goodness happens.

But the initial question remains—how to teach springtime to ice and sand? For this the words of knowledge are useless. It would be necessary to make *ipês* sprout in ice and sand! And I know only one word that has the power: the word of the poets. Teach solidarity? May the words of poets be heard in churches, in schools, in companies, in houses, on television, in bars, at political meetings, and, mainly, in loneliness…

"The child looked at me with beseeching eyes

And all of a sudden, I was a boy who looked with beseeching eyes."

Three Causes

Though he earns his living as a goldsmith, everybody knows that by the grace of God he was born a musician. It was fair then that everybody called him "Maestro" Tonico, though his complete name was Antônio Martins de Araújo. I personally examined the instruments of his work, evidence that he wasn't just a legendary figure. They were the instruments of a tinker, a peasant. Most significant is the faithful tuning fork that today continues to vibrate the *la* the same way the maestro made it vibrate in Goiás Velho, the city where he lived. It isn't the instrument that makes a musician, it's the ear, and the ear of Maestro Tonico was perfect.

Music was so strong in Maestro Tonico's body that all of his six children were born musicians. The most probable explanation for this apparent coincidence is that, perhaps, at the supreme moment of the act of love, the maestro must have been dreaming of another song. Violin, clarinet, flute, mandolin, zither, and cello made up a beautiful domestic orchestra. And that was the supreme happiness of Maestro Tonico—to see his children together, in tune with each other, playing under the direction of his baton.

Johann Sebastian Bach had something to do with our Maestro Tonico. He was a modest organist in a city of the countryside. He never had fame or recognition. One of his patrons once referred to him in a letter as a "mediocre musician." As a weekly duty he had to compose sacred works for the liturgy of the Lutheran service. His compositions, once performed, were forgotten and stored in baskets and on shelves in some room of the church. When Bach was surprised by death in the middle of *Art of the Fugue*, no one paid any mind to what he had written. His manuscripts were sold to a butcher to use to wrap meat. Mendelssohn, by chance, went to buy meat from that butcher. But he soon lost interest in meat, shocked by what he saw written on the paper in which he saw it being wrapped. And so it was that Bach was discovered in the most depressing place in the world: wrapping meat in a butcher shop. Thank God Mendelssohn wasn't a vegetarian!

A similar thing happened with the compositions of Maestro Tonico, without a similarly happy ending. After his death, the trunk where he stored his compositions was

27

transferred to one of those dark cellars that were common in the old wattle-and-daub houses. It happened that someone left the cellar door open. A goat ignorant of music walked in and devoured all the compositions of Maestro Tonico.

Beautiful, truly, was the death of the maestro. Sick with cancer, suffering, weak, he was surrounded by his family. Goiás Velho, like all towns of traditional culture, had a bandstand where the town band gave concerts. The music could be heard from the agonizing maestro's room. Suddenly, Maestro Tonico, until then indifferent, stirred himself, gesturing that he wanted to speak. Everyone moved close, ears piqued. One of his sons held his head, and he muttered, "The clarinet is out of tune at B-flat." That said, he delivered his soul to God. He couldn't allow his death to be bothered by a B-flat out of tune.

I carry sadness because many of the things that live within me cannot be communicated. The more I talk and explain, the more those who listen don't understand. It's like the oxcart. Those who don't know think that the oxcart was a means of primitive transportation. Those who know know that the oxcart, before being a means of transportation, was a musical instrument. It begins with the shape. Seen from above, its body appears to be the body of a violin. The driver drove to make the oxcart sing.[1] He

28

---

1   Rustic Brazilian oxcarts had wooden wheels and axles. The wagon was supported by forked wood that straddled the axle. As the axle turned, the friction created a moaning sound.

even threw water on the axle so the music became more strained. It was lament without end, a passionate moaning. Zeca Carreiro drove an oxcart in Mossâmedes, a city in the outback of Goiás state. As he approached town, he hurried up, throwing water on the axle so the lament of his cart would be heard and experienced by everyone. "It's singing with passion," he said proudly. And that's how he came into town, with the pride of a great musician who know how to play his instrument.

Time passed. Zeca Carreiro was hit with a malady that hits many musicians—deafness. Like Beethoven, Zeca Carreiro no longer heard the music that his oxcart played. But he still drove his cart, had to drive it. It was his livelihood. His grandson helped him, going ahead of the oxen as a guide. Approaching town, not hearing anything, he asked his grandson, "Zinho, is the cart singing?"

"It is, gramps," the grandson confirmed with a gesture.

"Is it singing with passion?" the grandfather continued. The boy smiled, and the grandfather understood. Zeca Carreira sat up straight like in the old days and came into town like the conductor of an orchestra.

Herodiano—that was his name. What strange idea led someone to baptize their young son in homage to the king who killed children—Herod! But the name did not

29

influence him. He was a gentle and happy person. Everyone liked him and called by the nickname Diano. He was in school only to the third grade, but he studied on his own. He liked literature, theater, and he was snobbish in the expensive French restaurants of Rio. That was because, by luck and effort, he became rich, very rich. He was even the owner of a silent movie cinema, the cultural center of the town of Dores. This was in the 1920s. It happened that, unexpectedly, a young artistic couple arrived in Dores. She was a young blonde from the capital. In Dores there was neither hotel nor boarding house. The couple stayed at Diano's house. They wanted to put on an art show. They rented the cinema. Since Dores was a small town, the men were excited by the blonde. The women were jealous, and they got mad at the men. It was rather unlikely that the cinema would fill. Diano imagined the two before an empty auditorium. He felt bad. And he made a decision of a rich man who can afford to throw away money. He bought from himself every seat in the house and passed out tickets for free. The theater filled. The show was a success. The young couple were enchanted. They left Dores happy, their pocketbook full. They never suspected what had happened. The name of the man, I do not know. The name of the woman was Dercy Gonçalves. She still doesn't know what happened. I know because the one who told me was Diano, my father.

Popcorn

Cooking fascinates me. Once in a while I even dare to try it. But the fact is, I am more competent with words than with pots and pans. For that reason I've written more about cooking than actually cooking. I dedicate myself to something that could be called "literary culinary." I've written about a great variety of entities in the world of the kitchen: onions, ora-pro-nobis, chopped beef with tomato, rice and beans, cod, soufflés, soups, barbecue. I even reached the point of dedicating half of a philo-poetical book to a meditation on the film *Babette's Feast*, which is a celebration of food as a ritual of sorcery. Aware of my limitations and competences, I have never written as a chef. I wrote as a philosopher, poet, psychoanalyst, and theologian—because the culinary stimulates all those functions of thought.

31

Foods, for me, are dream entities. They stimulate my capacity to dream. At the same time, I never imagined that the day would come when popcorn would make me dream. But that's precisely what happened. Popcorn—dried corn, tough, rounded grains—always seemed to me a simple little joke, a delicious game, without metaphysical or psychoanalytical dimension. But a few days ago I was talking with a patient who mentioned popcorn. And something unexpected happened in my mind. My ideas began to pop like popcorn. Then I saw a metaphoric relationship between popcorn and the act of thinking. A good thought is born like an unexpected, unforeseen burst of popcorn. So popcorn revealed itself to me like an extraordinary poetic object. Poetic because as I thought about popcorn my thoughts started popping and jumping around like the kernels in the pot.

I remembered the religious meaning of popcorn. Popcorn has a religious meaning? For Christians, the sacraments are bread and wine, which symbolize the body and blood of Christ, a mixture of life and joy (because life, life alone, without joy, is not life...). Bread and wine should be taken together. Life and joy should exist together. So I am reminded of the lesson I learned with Mother Stella, the powerful Bahian candomblé wise-woman: that popcorn is a sacred candomblé[2] food.

32

---

2   Candomblé is a syncretic religion brought to Brazil from Africa by slaves and modified to adopt certain elements of Catholicism.

Popcorn is a withered, underdeveloped corn. If I were an ignorant farmer, and if some of these runty spigots appeared among my full-blown corn, I'd get mad and get rid of them. From the perspective of size, popcorn can't compete with normal corn. I don't know how this happened, but the fact is that someone had the idea of shucking the spigots and putting the kernels in a pan over a fire, expecting the kernels to get soft so they could be eaten. After the experiment with water failed, they tried with oil. What happened next, no one would ever have imagined. All of a sudden the kernels began to burst, jumping in the pan with an enormous noise. But the extraordinary thing was what happened to them: tough, tooth-breaking kernels turned into soft, white flowers that even children could eat. Thus the bursting of the kernels went from a simple culinary operation to a party, a game, foolishness that everyone, especially children, laughed at. It's very funny to see corn popping!

And what does this have to do with candomblé? It's that the transformation of hard corn into soft popcorn is a symbol of the great transformation that all people should go through so they can be what they ought to be. The popcorn kernel isn't all it ought to be. It ought to be that which happens after the pop. The kernel is us: hard tooth-breakers inappropriate for consumption. By the power of fire we can, all of a sudden, transform ourselves into something else.

We can return to being children!

But the transformation takes place only under the force of fire. Kernels that don't pass through fire go on being kernels forever. That's what happens to people. The great transformations happen when we pass through fire. Whoever doesn't pass through fire remains the same their whole lives. They are people of a sameness and an astonishing hardness. It's just that they don't realize it. They think their way of being is the best way to be. But all of a sudden there's fire. Fire is when life thrusts us into a situation we never imagined. Pain. It could be fire from outside: to lose love, lose a child, get sick, lose a job, become poor. It could be fire from inside. Panic, fear, anxiety, depression—sufferings whose causes we do not know. There is always recourse in medicine. To put out the fire. Without fire, the suffering diminishes, and with it the possibility of transformation.

I imagine that the poor popcorn, closed up in a pot, thinking, as it gets hotter inside, that its time has come, that it's going to die. From inside its hard shell, closed up inside itself, it can't imagine any other end. It can't imagine the transformation that is being prepared. It doesn't imagine what it is capable of. Then, without warning, under the force of fire, the great transformation happens: Pop! And it looks like something else, something completely different, something it had never dreamed. It's the ugly, crawling caterpillar coming out of its cocoon as a flying butterfly.

In Christian symbology, the miracle of popcorn is represented by the death and resurrection of Christ. The resurrection is the popping of a kernel. You have to stop being one way to be another. "Die and transform yourself!" Goethe wrote.

In the state of Minas Gerais, everybody knows what *piruá* is. Talking about *piruás* with some people from the state of São Paulo, I discovered that they don't know what *piruás* are. Some even think I was kidding, that *piruá* is a nonexistent word. I found myself forced to check the *Aurélio* dictionary to confirm my knowledge of the language. A *piruá* is a popcorn kernel that has refused to pop. My friend William, an extraordinary research professor at Unicamp— the federal university at Campinas, São Paulo—who is a specialist in the area of corn, unveiled the wonder of popcorn popping. He certainly has a scientific explanation for *piruás*. But in the world of poetry, scientific explanations don't count. For example, in Minas Gerais, *"piruás"* is the name that they give to women who never marry. *Old maids.* My cousin, over forty, laments, "I've become a *piruá!*" but I think the metaphorical power of *piruás* is much greater. Old maids are those who refuse to change no matter how much they are scorched by fire. They think that there can be nothing more wonderful than the way they are. They ignore what Jesus said: "Whoever preserves their life loses

35

it."

Their presumption and their fear are the hard shell of the kernel that doesn't pop. Their fate is sad. They will remain hard their entire lives. They won't give happiness to anyone. When the joyous popping is done, in the bottom of the pot remain the old kernels who were never good for anything. Their destiny is the trash.

As for the kernels that pop, they are adults who go back to being children and who know that life is a big game...

Mental Health

I was invited to give a lecture about mental health. The people who invited me supposed that I, as a psychoanalyst, ought to be a specialist in the subject. And I thought so, too. So much so that I accepted. But as soon as I stopped and thought about it, I regretted my decision. I saw that I didn't know anything. Let me explain.

I began my thoughts by making a list of people who, in my point of view, have had a rich and exciting mental life, people whose books and projects are food for my soul. Nietzsche, Fernando Pessoa, Van Gogh, Wittgenstein, Cecília Meireles, Vladimir Mayakovski. And then I was shocked. Nietzsche went crazy. Fernando Pessoa was given to drink. Van Gogh killed himself. Wittgenstein was happy to know he would die soon; he no longer tolerated living with such angst. Cecília Meirles suffered chronic light

37

depression. Mayakovski committed suicide. All of them were profound, lucid people who will continue to be bread for the living long after we have been completely forgotten.

But did they have mental health? Mental health— that condition in which ideas behave themselves, always balanced, foreseeable, without surprises, obedient to the commands of duty, everything in its place like soldiers in rank order, never allowing the body to miss work or do something unexpected. It isn't necessary to take a trip around the world in a sailboat. It's enough to do what Shirley Valentine did. (If you haven't seen the film yet, do.) Or have a prohibited love affair, or, more dangerous than all of this, the courage to think what's never been thought. Thinking is a dangerous thing…

No, mental health they did not have. They were too lucid for that. They knew that the world is controlled by crazy old people in neckties. Being owners of power, the crazy go on to become the prototypes of mental health. Of course none of the names I cited would survive the tests that psychologists would have subjected them to if they were to look for employment in a company. On the other hand, I've never heard of a politician who had stress or depression. They always go parading around the streets of town, passing out smiles and certainties.

I feel like my thoughts are the thoughts of a crazy person, so let me hurry on to some obligatory clarifications.

We are very much like computers. The function of the computer, as everybody knows, requires the interaction of two parts. One of them is called hardware, literally the hard equipment, and the other is called software. The hardware consists of all the solid things that the appliance is made of. The software is made up of "spiritual" entities—symbols that form the programs and are recorded on discs. We, too, have hardware and software. The hardware are the nerves of the brain, the neurons—everything that makes up the nervous system. The software is made up of a series of applications that are recorded in our memory. Just as in computers, what remains in the memory are symbols, gossamer-light entities that could be said to be "spiritual," the most important application being language. A computer can go crazy through a flaw in its hardware or its software. So can we. When our hardware goes crazy, we call in the psychiatrists and neurologists, who come in with their chemical potions and scalpels to fix what went bad. When the problem is in our software, however, potions and scalpels don't work. You can't fix an application with a screwdriver. Since software is made of symbols, only symbols can get into it. To deal with software, you have to make use of symbols. For that reason, whoever deals with disturbances in human software never sees anything good in physical resources. Their tools are words, and they may be poets, humorists, clowns, writers, gurus, friends, or even

39

psychoanalysts. It happens, though, that this computer that is the human body has a peculiarity that differentiates it from others. Its hardware, the body, is sensitive to things that the software produces. And isn't that what happens to us? We hear a song and we cry. We read Drummond's erotic poems and the body gets excited. Imagine a sound system. Imagine that the record player and accessories, the hardware, had the capacity to hear the music that it played and to be emotionally moved. And imagine that the beauty is so great that the hardware doesn't behave and breaks down with emotion! Well that's what happened with those people I cited at the beginning. The music that came out of their software was so beautiful that their hardware couldn't stand it. Given these theoretical presuppositions, we are now in a position to offer a recipe that will guarantee, for those who accept the risk, mental health until the end of their days. Opt for modest software. Avoid beautiful and emotionally moving things. Beauty is dangerous to hardware. Be careful with music. Brahms and Mahler are especially contraindicated. Rock can be taken at will. As for readings, avoid those that make you think. There is a vast literature specializing in impeding thought. If there are books by Dr. Lair Ribeiro,[3] why risk reading Saramago? Newspapers have the same effect. They should be read daily. Since they publish the same things every day with

40

---

3   Brazilian cardiologist and internationally renowned author of self-help books for executives.

different names and faces, it is guaranteed that our software will always think the same things. And on Sundays, don't forget Silvio Santos and Gugu Liberato.[4] Following this recipe, you will have a banal but tranquil life. But since you have cultivated insensibility, you will not sense how banal it is. And instead of reaching the end that the people I mention reached, you will retire to realize your dreams. Unfortunately, however, when you arrive at that moment, you will have forgotten what they were.

41

4   Sílvio Santos is the Brazilian host of an interminable Sunday television program of pop culture. Liberato was his producer and also a television personality.

On Politics and Gardening

*O*f all the vocations, politics is the most noble. Vocation: from the latin *vocare*, "calling." Vocation is an inner call of love. Not love for a man or woman but for a *thing-to-be-done*. This *thing-to-be-done* marks the place where the called want to make love with the world. There, in the place of their *thing-to-be-done,* they want to penetrate, ejaculate, fecundate. Psychology of the lover: to do without wishing to gain. To do even if their *thing-to-be-done* puts them in danger. Many lovers have died because of ephemeral moments of pleasure with a prohibited love.

Political vocation is a passion for a garden. Let me explain. "Politics" comes from *polis*, city. A city was, for the Greeks, a safe place, orderly and tame, where men could dedicate themselves to the pursuit of happiness. Political vocation, then, is at the service of citizens' happiness, the happiness of people in the city.

To the contrary of the Greeks, for the Hebrews this living space was not represented by the city. God did not create a city, he created a garden. Their God was not an urbanist; he was a gardener, an inventor of paradises. Perhaps it was by the fact that they'd been nomads in the desert. Those who live in a desert dream of oases. So the garden, for the Hebrews, was that which the *polis* was for the Greeks. If we asked a Hebrew prophet "What is politics?" he would respond, "The art of gardening applied to public things."

Vocational politicians are in love with a big garden that's for everyone. Their love is so great that they give up the little garden that they could till for themselves. What good is a little garden if all around you is a desert? The whole desert needs to be turned into a garden.

I love my vocation, which is to write. But I know that the beauty of literature is weak. A little poem by Emily Dickenson:

> *To make a prairie, it takes a clover and a bee,*
> *One clover, and a bee.*
> *And reverie.*
> *The reverie alone will do,*
> *If bees are few.*

43

It would be good if it were true. But the fact is, fantasies aren't enough to plant gardens. To turn into gardens, fantasies need bees: hands, tools, power. But power is what the poet does not have. But the politicians do. Politicians by vocation are poets with power. They have the power to dig, plant, care for, pull up, prune, make walls. Politicians make laws and take measures for them to be obeyed. The nobility of the political vocation is in that it has the power to transform the dream of a garden into a real garden where life takes place.

It is such a pleasing vocation that Plato suggested that politicians do not need to possess anything as private property. It doesn't make sense to have a private garden when you're the gardener of the big garden. For that reason it would be undignified for the gardener to have a privileged space better or different than the space occupied by everyone else. Laws for the politician are laws for everyone. I know, and have known, many vocational politicians. Their lives were and continue to be a reason for hope.

Vocation is different from profession. In a vocation, the person finds happiness in the act itself. In a profession, pleasure is found not in the act but in the gain derived. The professional who is only professional does his *thing-to-be-done* not for the love of it but for the love of something outside of it: the salary, the gain, the profit, the advantage. People motivated by vocation are lovers. Professionals, to the contrary, don't love their lovers; they use them for their own advantage. They are gigolos.

All vocations can be turned into professions. Prophets are followed by mercenaries. Gardeners by vocation give their lives to everyone else's garden. Gardeners by profession use everyone else's garden to build their own garden even though, for this to happen, the desert and the suffering around them must increase.

Thus it is with politics. There are many professional politicians. So therefore I utter my second thesis: Of all the professions, professional politics is the most vile. This explains people's total disenchantment with politics. No one believes what politicians say.

Guimarães Rosa, asked by Günter Lorenz whether he considered himself political, responded:

> I could never be a politician with all the charlatanism of reality… Politicians are always talking about reason, logic, reality, and things like that and at the same time practicing the most irrational acts imaginable. Unlike "legitimate" politicians, I believe in mankind and I wish us a future. The politician thinks only in minutes. I am a writer, and I think in eternities. I think about the resurrection of man.

Anyone who think in minutes doesn't have the patience to plant trees. A tree takes many years to grow. It is much more profitable to cut them down.

Our future depends on a struggle between politicians by vocation and politicians by profession. The sad thing is that many who feel the calling of politics do not have the courage to attend to it in fear of the shame of having to get along with gigolos. I'm one—but now it's too late.

I speak to you, the young, to seduce you into becoming gardeners. Maybe there's a dormant politician inside you (like in the story of *Sleeping Beauty*). Hearing the vocation is hard because it is disturbed by the noise of the expected choices: teaching, medicine, engineering, computing, law, science. All of them are legitimate if they are vocations. But they are all funneling: They all put you into a little corner of the garden that's far from the place where the fate of the garden is decided. Wouldn't it be a lot more fascinating to take part in the fate of the garden?

We recently celebrated 500 years since the discovery of Brazil. The discoverers, when they arrived, didn't find a garden. They found a jungle. A jungle isn't a garden. Jungles are cruel and insensitive, indifferent to suffering and death. A jungle is a part of nature still not touched by the hand of man. That jungle could have been transformed into a garden. It hasn't been. The politicians that attended to it were not lovers. They were woodchoppers. Gigolos. And that's how the jungle, which could have been turned into a garden for the happiness of all, was transformed into deserts flecked with luxurious private gardens where a few found life and pleasure.

There are discoveries of origins. More beautiful are discoveries of destinies.

So maybe, if the politicians of vocation take possession of the garden, we can begin to write a new history that does not repeat the past but a history that celebrates the future. But this can only happen if the woodchoppers are thrown out and replaced by gardeners. So instead of deserts and private gardens we would have a big garden for everyone,. It would be the work people who loved to plant trees in whose shade they would never sit and who would feed themselves with food that birds brought from the future (Nietzsche). We would have the happiness of seeing men, women and children living and playing in a garden...

The Dumbed-down House

With your permission, I say: for thinking far ahead, I
am a bloodhound—if you release before me a slight idea, I
will track it into the deepest forest, amen!

*I*t was Riobaldo who said that.[5] I agree and say amen. Because I was tracking some dumbed-down mice raised by professor Tsien and some theories of professor Reuben Feuerstein in the middle of a dense forest of ideas when I bumped into a boy in flip-flop sandals at the door of the Guarapuava Airport, which stopped my tracking in its tracks. What he asked me for was more important. He asked me to buy a homemade snack to help him out. I stopped, bought one, ate it, lost track of where I was

5   In *The Devil to Pay in the Backlands*, by Guimarães Rosa, Riobaldo is a rural peasant who often makes philsophical statements in a dialect unique to the northeast region.

and stopped tracking the mice of professor Tsien and the theories of professor Feuerstein. I went into a "digression." My thoughts took an excursion through the flavors of my emotions—but now I'm back, and the bloodhound has caught the scent again.

So, professor Tsien, of Princeton University, set himself to working on raising mice that were dumber than trained mice. If you are surprised by a scientist spending time and money on producing dumbed-down mice, I wish to call your attention to the fact that idiocy is quite useful from the social and political point of view. Aldous Huxley said that the social stability of the Brave New World is due to the psycho-pedagogical mechanisms whose objective was to dumb people down. Education worked for a variety of ends. Intelligent people, who live thinking and having different ideas, are dangerous. To the contrary, the socio-political order is better served by people who always think the same thoughts, that is, dumbed-down people. Because being dumb is just this: to think the same thoughts—even if they are grandiose thoughts. Proof of that are the societies of bees and ants, notable for their stability and capacity to survive.

49

Professor Tsien's dumbed-down mice, confronted with problematic situations, were always routed by trained mice. But the objective of the research was intelligent. Professor Tsien wanted to test a theory: whether dumb mice, if put into interesting, stimulating, challenging situations, would use their inferior intelligence to construct mechanisms that made them more intelligent. In other words, genetic limitations of intelligence would be compensated by challenges in the environment. So he put the dumb mice in cages that looked more like amusement parks with dozens of things to be done, dozens of situations to be explored, dozens of curious objects. Just like idiots who are curious and live to mess around with things, the mice began to act. After a little while, put into identical situations with trained mice, the dumb mice stopped being dumb. They didn't recover their ignorance.

I don't know the work of professor Feuerstein. His theories on intelligence were told to me. I was fascinated. I hope he's right. Because what he thinks crosses the laboratory conclusions of professor Tsien. Feuerstein has special interest in people who, through genetic factors (Down Syndrome, for example) or environmental factors (environments culturally and economically poor) had their intelligence compromised. In tests, their performance is inferior to that of "normal" children. His hypothesis, tested and confirmed, is that, if these people were in places in interesting, challenging, varying environments, their inferior intelligence would undergo a transformation for the better. Intelligence was fed by challenge. Confronted with challenges, it grew and flourished.

Without challenges, it wilted and shrank. Privileged intelligence can also be dumbed-down by the lack of stimulation and challenge. This led me to make a leap from professor Tsien's mice and professor Feuerstein's theories to the houses where we live. Our houses are one of the many environments in which we live. Each environment is a stimulus to the intelligence. (It's hard to be intelligent in an elevator. In the elevator, there's only one thing to do: push a button.) And I thought that there are houses that dumb down, and there are houses where intelligence can flourish. It doesn't help for the houses to be designed by architects, abundant and decorated by professionals, full of objets d'art. I don't know if decoration is art that was learned in school. If decoration is learned in school, I ask whether there exists, in the curriculum, a subject with the title "Decorating to Dumb Down—Decorating to Prod Intelligence." This question isn't an idle thought. Houses that dumb down make disagreeable people. Such houses create tedium. I imagine that many marital conflicts and separations are due to the fact that their house, finely decorated, dumbs down the residents. Objects there can't be touched. Everything has to be in order, a place for each thing, each thing in its place. The house is in perfect order, the pride of the housewife.

I think it was Jaspers who said that you don't need to travel because everything worth knowing is in your house.

Jasper traveled without leaving home. But there are houses that are tedium: a place to sleep, to take a bath, to eat, to watch television. If that's what a house is, then, after sleeping, taking a bath, eating and watching television, there is nothing else to do in the house, and the remedy is to leave the disagreeable cage and go other places where interesting things can be found. I suggest to psycho-pedagogists that, when working with a child supposedly a little dumb, they investigate the house where the child lives. The most fascinating room in my grandfather's old colonial townhouse was the mysterious room, entry prohibited, where odds and ends and useless things accumulated over a century were stored in total disarray. There my imagination ran loose. But the parlor, beautiful and decorated, was boring. Children never spent time there. In the parlor the only thing that fascinated me were the sleek, imported, colored windows through which the sun filtered. In my experience, intelligence begins in the hands. Children don't satisfy themselves with sight. They want to pick up, turn around, manipulate, take apart, put together. Is a lover satisfied with the act of seeing the body of the beloved? Why, then, should intelligence be satisfied with the act of seeing things? The purpose of the eyes is to show the hands the path to things to be messed with.

I think a house should be full of objects to be messed with. The house itself is to be messed with. That's why I prefer old houses. I have a friend who bought a beautiful apartment, brand new, and he's dying of boredom. Because in his apartment there is nothing to be fixed. I feel a certain discreet happiness when something breaks or goes on the fritz. Because then I get to play...

Books need to be within reach of hands. Everywhere. In the living room, bathroom, kitchen, bedroom. A small bookshelf near the toilet is very useful for quickly reading books. Art books, for example! It's important that children and young adults learn that books are worlds through which we make delightful excursions. Of course! For this, there must be guides. Be careful with toys. A toy is an object that challenges our ability with our hands and with our ideas. Toys that need only the push of a button to make something happen are dumb-down objects—push the button, the doll sings; push the other button, the doll pees; push a button, the car goes. They don't make us think. As soon as the girl decides to do surgery on the doll to see how the magic happens—at that moment she will start becoming smart. Puzzles—wonderful objects that develop an enormous variety of logical and aesthetic functions at the same time. Putting together a puzzle at night is an excellent form of family and pedagogical therapy. It's the parent teaching a child tricks. Tools are another. With tools children develop manual abilities, learn physics, and experience the pleasure of fixing or making things. The

53

amount of knowledge of mechanical physics that exists in a box of tools is incalculable. The kitchen open to everyone. It's a wonderful laboratory of chemistry. Cooking educates sensibility.

You have never thought of that, the relation between your house and your intelligence, your intelligence and that of your children. Your house can be a dumber-downer. Or it can be a fascinating place where professor Tsien's mice suddenly become smart...

When Pain Turns into Poetry

Today, Friday, September 20, 1996, my desire is to not write.

I write like a sleepwalker, perhaps in the hope that words might succeed in diminishing my pain. But I don't want the pain to diminish. I don't want to be cured. I don't want to be consoled. I don't want to become happy again. When pain dies down it's because forgetfulness has done its job. But I don't want to forget. Love can't stand forgetfulness.

Empty of the words that pain stole, the soul returns to poets. In truth, it isn't quite like that. The soul doesn't return to anything. It is embraced by its pain. It is poets who come to our aid, even without being called. That's the vocation of poets: to put words in places where the pain is too bad. Not to end it but so it can turn into something eternal: a star

55

in the firmament, shining sans surcease in the dark night. That's what love desires—to eternalize pain, turning it into something beautiful. When this happens, pain turns into poetry, an object of communion, a sacrament.

The pain is such that the search for words—pure toys when they're happy—becomes an enormous weight, a ball of iron dragged along, a stone rolled to the top of the mountain knowing that the effort is useless because it will roll back down. I feel an enormous laziness, a somnolent half-heartedness for writing. I drag myself. I oblige myself to drag. I push the words like someone pushing blocks of granite. I'd really like to be still, to not say anything, to not write anything. Might there be a publication that accepts an essay that's just a blank page, pure silence? I write to shut myself up, to produce silence. As in a Gothic cathedral the walls, pillars, and windows serve only to create an empty space where one can pray. Álvaro de Campos understands that poetry is just that, an edifice of words in whose nooks another voice is heard, a song that makes you cry.

I know my words are useless. Death makes everything useless. I look around at the things I love, the things that give me happiness—garden, water well, CDs, artwork, wine. Ah! His laugh was a waterfall when he was opening a bottle of wine! Everything is gray, nothing shines, all without color, without taste. I don't open the wine. I know it turned to vinegar. I water my plants in obligation. Duty pushes me: they need me. I thank my dog in obligation, too. He isn't guilty. I answer the telephone, and I am gentle with people who speak with me. They have yet to receive the news that they will receive. I tried to give the news to a few people. I tell them that I've been crying for six hours without stopping. They laugh. Not in malice but because they think I'm kidding.

My best friend died. So all words are useless. Over the waterfall of his laugh is written, "Nevermore." None of them can fill the void. I recollect Cecília's words—words which, I believe, were written long after the pain, after the pain had turned into beauty.

> (...) But all is useless because your ears are like conches, empty, and your immovable nostril no longer takes in the news of the world that circulates in the wind (...) But all is useless because you lying on cool earth, and your eyes don't look for more places in this luminous scene, and your hands don't reach out for the harvest or a caress.

My best friend. A friend is a person who, just because you remember him, brings out a happy laugh. That's how friends are—none are more of a friend or less of a friend. Either they are or they aren't. They're all equal. But I know that my other friends will understand me when I tell them

Best Chronicles

Elias Abrahão was my best friend. If you have ten children and one dies, that was the one you loved the most. If a shepherd has a hundred sheep and one gets lost, that was the one he liked the most. Elias died. He was my best friend. My body and my soul, today, are a vessel filled with the pain of its emptiness.

The poet W.H. Auden once said exactly what I'm feeling:

Stop all the clocks, cut off the telephone,
Prevent the dog from barking with a juicy bone,
Silence the pianos and with muffled drum
Bring out the coffin, let the mourners come.

Let aeroplanes circle moaning overhead
Scribbling on the sky the message He Is Dead,
Put crepe bows round the white necks of the public doves,
Let the traffic policemen wear black cotton gloves.

He was my North, my South, my East and West,
My working week and my Sunday rest,
My noon, my midnight, my talk, my song
I thought that love would last for ever: I was wrong.

The stars are not wanted now: put out every one;
Pack up the moon and dismantle the sun;
Pour away the ocean and sweep up the wood.
For nothing now can ever come to any good.

At moments like this I have immense pity on people who

have a strong god. Because, poor things, they are lost in the face of death.

To have a strong god is to know that, if he had wanted, he could have prevented the death. If he didn't prevent it, it was because he didn't want to. Now, if he was the one who killed him, he can't be suffering. He's happy for having done what he did. So, he is to blame for my pain. He and I are very distant, infinitely distant. How could I love him, a god so cruel? But, if he is a weak god, that means that he wasn't the one who ordered it. He could not have prevented it. A weak god can cry with me. He can even excuse himself: "It wasn't possible to prevent it. I know because I tried. Look at these wounds on my body. They prove that I tried…." He cries with me. So the two of us, my god and I, cry together. And that's why we love each other.

In my backyard there's a tree, a sandalwood with a delightful fragrance. It was Elias who gave me the seedling. It came from Lebanon. I will take care of it with redoubled attention. Once in a while I will water it with wine. It will not surprise me if it gets drunk and starts to laugh. I'll know that Elias is nearby.

Candles

*C*hristmas is coming. I'm scared. Scared of the insanity. Christmas is a time when people get all bothered. They sing *Silent Night*. But their bodies and souls are at war, possessed by agitation and rush. When Baby Jesus was born, the Devil ran away. I make use of candles to exorcise insanity. For a whole year I have left them forgotten in the dark of a cabinet. A puff of my breath put them to sleep. And asleep they have stayed, like Sleeping Beauty, waiting for the flame that would awaken them. They look dead. But I know that a touch of fire will bring them to life again. They await resurrection. How human they are! They look like us. Our hardened bodies, too, can burn again. All they need is to be touched by the magic of fire!

I need them, my candles. Their faithful flames calm me. "Do you want to become calm?" old Gaston Bachelard asked. "Breathe softly before the delicate candle as it calmly performs the work of illumination."

So different from lamps! Would it be possible, perchance, to love a lamp? What tame emotions might be born of its strong and indifferent light? Who would call those emotions up from my lamp? All lamps are the same. When they burn out, they inspire no sadness, only the inconvenience of exchanging them for others.

Candles are different. They cry while they illuminate. Their tears, born of fire, spill over and run down their body. They cry because they know that, to shine, they must die. It's impossible to contemplate a candle in its work of illumination without feeling a little sad. Its flame, modest, softened by indecision and tremors, makes me reflect back on myself. I'm the same. My flame vacillates when touched by the wind. That's why I can call the candle mine. We are made of the same substance. We have a fate in common. Candles tell different stories. Each one has a name that is its alone. One of them I stuck in the mouth of an empty wine bottle. Its colored tears ran down the glass and hardened. No handkerchief will dry them up. They stay there like memories of past moments that took place within its light and intimacy. Presences of an absence, lost time crystallized... My attentive gaze passes over their wrinkles. I note that there are various colors. That wine bottle has already held several candles. Green, red, and yellow tears mix and cover each other in a fabric of wax—generations that consumed themselves in the same fate of gently glowing. I look for the candle that ought to be there to be awakened. I see that she no longer exists. She was consumed, consumed until her last bit melted. She didn't spill a single tear. She simply fell into the bottle and disappeared. I see the female form of the bottle. It's a uterus with its vaginal opening pointed high, like the steeple of a cathedral.

I thought that maybe the candle was telling me that dying is like a disinclination to be born, a return to the maternal womb. I was touched because, in fact, a light that lit in moments passed stopped lighting. It had sunk into the bottle. That candle would never again be lit. All that's left is the memory of its moments of light. I think about what I should do. Leave the bottle as it is, with its colorful tears and emptiness? Or put another candle in there? No, the beauty of that bottle is due to precisely the testimony of successive generations that left their lives engraved on the glass. The flame must continue to shine. When a candle finishes, another must take its place.

A different candle is ashamed to cry. It hides inside a metal cup that doesn't let its tears overflow. It cries quietly, without flaunting. Blocked from overflowing, its tears turn into a flat and luminous interior lake of melted wax where the flame is reflected. Weeping has that power. It can make light more luminous. The candle refuses to let go of its pain. It holds back its tears, keeps them tight to its body, embracing them, recognizing them as part of itself. That's what poets do. Their light is modest, hidden in metal, hiding from the eye. But their flesh of wax is full of the delicious fragrance of cinnamon. When she cries, the air fills with beauty. I think perhaps this candle was made for those who can't see. Her perfumed light calms even those who have their eyes closed.

I take another candle into my hands. It's almost as thick as the bottle. In its ochre wax an artist has engraved leaves and flowers in relief. Even unlit it's beautiful. Sensitive hands that touch it can feel the drawings. The weak flame melted its own body, drank its own flesh. The flame shines from inside the vessel that the flame opened. The sculpted skin, too far from the heat, survived intact. Contemplated from afar, it gives the impression of solidity and permanence. But all you have to do is light the flame to see its fragility. The more worn by its fire, the more its skin became translucent and the light is filtered through its ephemeral flesh. What a magnificent lesson for candles— only the bodies worn out by the fire of love can become transparent!

Love prefers the light of candles. Maybe because that's everything we wish for a beloved—that she or he be a soft light that helps us tolerate the terror of the night. Under the light of love that gently and patiently shines, the dark

63

no long scares us so. It's a silent night!

Don't let your candles go out! Darkness is lonely and sad! Touch them again with the flame of love!

Old Violins Play Music...

esus was wise. He knew the secrets of the human heart. Unsurpassable psychoanalyst, he said, "A good man out of the good treasure of the heart bringeth forth good things: and an evil man out of the evil treasure bringeth forth evil things." (Matthew 12:35) In other words: we always find what we're looking for. This applies to a reading of the Holy Scriptures. People who are full of fear, of vengeful sentiments, of authoritarianism, will find in the Bible threats, punishments, hells, a cruel and vengeful God that looks like them. All Gods are portraits of those who believe in them. It is possible to psychoanalyze a person by analyzing their religious thoughts and feelings. Those who are full of tender sentiments and who are therefore not motivated by fear—"There is no fear in love; but perfect love casteth out fear." (1 John 4:18)—will from their treasure bring forth ideas of beauty, goodness, and forgiveness. Their god looks a lot like a child, with no vengeance, punishment, or hell.

I say this so that people may take something from the Holy Scriptures when they think about sex. A text comes to mind, inspired like all the others, in which the last moments of King David are described. In this event, related in the first verses of the Book of Kings, which I have never heard a sermon about, King David is already old. All his blankets were useless for keeping him warm. So his servants had a therapeutic idea: "Go get for our lord and king a young virgin to help the king and take care of him. He will sleep on her breast, and our lord and king will be warm." Thus it was done. But it was futile. It was futile for the king to sleep beside the most beautiful young girl in the kingdom. His body, once the body of a virile man— remember Bathsheba?—was not inert. The hope that he would be brought back to life by the pleasures of a woman did not go anywhere. He did not make love with her. What a deception! He died. What this sacred text says is that there was a conviction, shared by all, that sexual love has the power to perform the miracle of curing the body. Sex heats up the cold life. Sex is a remedy. Sex is happiness. (Those who only take bad things from their treasure will conclude, to the contrary, that sex is venom.)

One of my favorite texts is called *Desiderata.*

Desiderata means "bunch of things that are desired." There it is written, like a desire, "Accept with elegance that counsel of years, graciously leaving behind the pleasures of youth." The sentiment isn't explicit. What I took from it was this: Since sexual pleasures are pleasures that common sense takes as pleasures of youth, the elderly must accept the limitations of old age with elegance, so they don't become ridiculous. In old age, the pleasures of sex also age. How ridiculous, David, uninterested in the embrace of a beautiful young girl...

It's true, the pleasures of old age aren't the same as the pleasures of youth. I wrote an essay about an elderly couple who had waited more than 50 years to marry. Once the man's wife had died, and the woman's husband had died, the widow and widower got together to live, in the little time they had left, the love that had been choked back. The old man, 80 years old, came back to life. His first wife had hated the violin. He loved violin. Result: to avoid vocalized noise, he left his violin in the closet for more than 50 years. Left aside, the strings of the violin snapped and stayed snapped... ah! What metaphoric sadness for the soul of that man, a violin impeded from making music. Touched by old-new love, the strings of the soul tuned themselves, the old violinist came back to life from the coffin where he'd been imprisoned, and he took to restoring the violin that had been in the closet. (Sometimes a violin is more

67

potent, sexually, than the body of a maiden...) And the old violin, forgotten among the pleasures of youth, began to play again. This metaphor makes me laugh with happiness. Could this be it? Could the body be a violin? Could the soul be a song? There is, in the annals of psychoanalysis, a report of a person who dreamed of playing the violin in public—and the meaning of the dream was "masturbate in public." I don't quite remember. If it wasn't quite like that, let my colleagues correct me for the benefit of readers. What interests us is the luscious metaphorical relationship between a musical instrument and the sexual instruments. In the end, to make love is always to play a duet. The two play each other so the duet sounds as it should.

And the love was enormous, in the short time it lasted. The violin couldn't stand the intensity of the sonata. It shattered before it got to the end. The old man died at 81. I wrote an essay about the incident. Because, some time later, I got a telephone call from a woman I didn't know. It was her! For 40 minutes she told me told me in all detail about the joy of the love that she and her beloved had lived. And, at the end of the conversation, she told me something so beautiful that every time I tell it, I cry with emotion: "So it is, professor. At our age, we don't mess around much [please, notice the "much"] with the sex thing. We live for tenderness."

Sex in old age is, in fact, much different from sex

in adolescence. Adolescents, in their normal state, are
drugged. Don't get me wrong! I'm not saying they are
snorting cocaine. I'm saying that they are, all of a sudden,
invaded by a volcano of hormones that they don't know,
uncontrollable demons that take possession of them,
lodging with a certain preference in certain parts of the
body which go into motion, painfully, independently of
their own will. St. Augustine, in his book *De Civitate Dei*,
had already observed this autonomy of the sexual organs,
which moved without the permission of reason, creating
very embarrassing situations, reason for which the Creator,
pitying man's shame, furnished an apron to hide his
uncontrolled genitalia. It became hell. I don't know about
women. I know that, for men sexual desire in adolescence
is a suffering. It doesn't die down. The curious thing is
that it breaks out gratuitously, without provocation by any
necessity. The adolescent doesn't need to see naked women,
porno films or just a libidinous thought. Sexual desire in the
adolescent is independent of any object. It is pure, crude,
irrational desire. For anyone who doesn't understand
what I'm saying, let me take advantage of a comparison.
Really, it seems like the desire to pee. The bladder swells,
swells, begins to hurt, the pain grows and grows, becomes
intolerable. There's no way around it. The bladder must be
emptied. And there's that pleasure, that happiness... The
act of peeing, when the bladder is full, really is comparable

to the boner and the orgasm in adolescence. I even believe that the analysis Freud did on sexual pleasure takes the act of peeing as a model. The object of pleasure isn't pleasure; it is being freed of pain, returning to equilibrium, to the Buddhistic experience of not desiring anything: Nirvana...

That passes. This state of hormonal disturbance doesn't last long. It's like a wild horse, out of control, on the loose, breaking down the fence, jumping the creek, getting bogged down in a puddle. Later, the wild horse, pure power, atomic explosion, destruction, takes on form. Da Vinci believed horses were the most beautiful animals, after certain humans. The wild power takes form, discovers its limits. Brute power is ugly. As Nietzsche said: "When power becomes graceful, beauty takes place." So sex arises in another form: tenderness. Now the aforementioned uncontrolled organs stop moving under their own will. They only move when stirred by the tenderness of beauty... Without the tenderness of beauty, they remain inert. Fools think it's impotence or frigidity. It's nothing.

Abelard and Heloise

It's a white marble tomb in the cemetery Père-La-Chaise in Paris. Under the protection of a canopy of open stonework, also of marble, they can be found in definitive form, modeled by memory, by night, by desire.

They lie side by side, in mortuary vestments, without touching each other, faces turned toward the sky, hands crossed over their chests, without desire. A sculptor sculpted them that way, conforming to the way religious tradition immobilized the dead. But if the choice were theirs, the sculpture would be something else—Rodin's *The Kiss*, their naked bodies in embrace. And the engraved words would be those of Drummond: "Love is the cousin of death, and the conqueror of death, even if it's slain (and it is slain) in every instance of love."[6]

71

---

6   Carlos Drummond de Andrade (1902—1987), poet and writer, considered by some to be the greatest poet of the Portuguese language.

That's how the tomb of Abelard and Heloise is. They loved in a manner passionate and impossible, irremediably separated one from the other by life in the hope that death would join them eternally.

Love favored by fortune does not turn into literature or art. *Romeo and Juliet, Tristan and Isolde, the Bridges of Madison County, Love Story*—heart-touching love is wounded love. Octavio Paz says, "Things and words bleed from the same wound." But happy love isn't wounded. How, then, can words bleed from it? Happy love does not speak; it acts. If I write about Abelard and Heloise it's because their history is a wound in my own flesh. Heloise was 17, Abelard 38. Twenty-one years separated them. Love doesn't know time's abysms.

Abelard (1079-1120) was nicknamed "Wandering Bird." An effulgent intellectual, a central character in philosophical discussions in Paris, he was the cause of envy, hatred, and passion. Here's how Heloise described him in a letter to him:

> *What kings, what philosophers ever had renown equal to yours? What country, what city, what village never showed impatience to see you? You appear in public? Everyone rushes to see you. You go away? Everyone tries to follow you with avid eyes. What wife, virgin, hasn't burned for you in your absence and ignited in your presence?*

You possess, above all, two qualities capable of conquering all women: the charm of words and the beauty of voice. I don't believe that any other philosopher has possessed them to such high degree.

Heloise, a young adolescent endowed with rare qualities of intelligence, lived in Paris in her uncle's house. He, wishing to give her the best education, hired Abelard as her intellectual tutor. But the philosophy lessons didn't last long. Soon the two were lost in love. And Abelard, a philosopher of incomparable logical rigor, turned into a poet. Heloise took care of his thoughts and his body and, from then on, according to his own confession, in him were found only "verses of love and nothing of the secrets of philosophy."

The uncle, upon discovering what was happening in his house, felt betrayed and became furious. He interrupted the "lessons" and prohibited them from seeing each other. Futilely. Distance doused nothing. It fanned the flames of love. Abelard himself comments: "The separation of bodies rose to the maximum the union of our hearts, and, because it wasn't quenched, our passion flared up more and more."

73

But Heloise got pregnant. Abelard decided to elope with her and take her somewhere far away. By night he got her from her uncle's house and took her to his sister's house in Palet, four hundred kilometers from Paris. And there the child of their love was born. They married secretly on July 30 of that year.

But for Heloise's uncle, the affair demanded revenge. So he planned the worst of all possible vengeance. He hired a band of thugs who invaded Abelard's house and castrated him. He thought that would put an end to the love. It was no use. They continued to love each other for the rest of their lives with the power of memory and longing—until death united them eternally. As in the film *The Bridges of Madison County*. Except that in the film, the instrument of castration wasn't the hatred of someone but the pious love of someone.

In 1142 Abelard died at the age of 63. Heloise, learning of his death, demanded possession of "her man" for herself. In fact, that was what Abelard had requested. "When I die," he wrote, "I ask you to have my body transported to the cemetery of your parish..." And Heloise demanded that after she died, her body should be buried in her husband's tomb. Which happened 21 years later.

It is said that, on being taken to the tomb, when Aberlard's coffin was opened, he opened his arms and embraced her. Others say that, to the contrary, it was Heloise who opened her arms to embrace him. It's possible. Perhaps Heloise's love had been more pure and intense. Abelard had known the love of many women and the love of philosophy. Heloise, on the other hand, knew only the love of Abelard. One of his biographies says: "For Heloise, there were only two events in her life: the day she knew she was loved by Abelard, and the day she lost him. Everything else disappears from her eyes in a deep night." Even today, after nine hundred years, lovers visit that tomb. Maybe to beseech God that they be eternally embraced, as in Rodin's The Kiss. Maybe to ask that we be given the happiness of living a love like that, but without living the pain. Love favored by fate, without literature, without fame, without anyone knowing. The illiterate happiness of "a homely little love," as Adélia Prado so lovingly baptized it, is enough for us. I am sure this is what Abelard and Heloise desired.

The Final Chord

I had put on the record player that record with the poems of Vinícius[7] and Drummond, an old long-play record, with its danger of scratches making the needle jump, but fortunately up till then everything was lovely and nice, with no jumps, no squeaks, and Vinícius himself, in his hoarse voice of whiskey and cigarettes, reciting the sonnets of separation, of leave-taking, of total love, the eyes of a lover. He had come to my favorite song, "The Having"—Vinícius was perceiving that night was coming, so he tried to weigh everything that he'd done and what remained of it. So the strophes all begin with the same word… "Remaining…" —that's what was left.

76

---

7   Vinícius de Morães was among the creators of bossa nova. He composed the lyrics of such classic songs as "Garota de Ipanema" (Girl from Ipanema), "Insensitáz" "How Insensitiv") and "Chega de Saudade" (No more Blues).

Remaining, above all, that capacity for tenderness, that perfect intimacy with the silence (…)

Remaining, that will to weep before beauty, that blind cholera in the face of injustice and misunderstanding (…

Remaining, that incoercible faculty of dreaming (…) and that tiny, indecipherable light to which poems sometimes give the name hope (…)

At that moment the last quatrain began, and after so many times that I've read it and heard it, I knew the color of his words, and they went repeating inside me, anticipating the last, which would be the end, knowing that all that is beautiful must end.

Sunset is beautiful because its colors are ephemeral and in a few minutes will cease to be.

The sonata is beautiful because its life is short. It doesn't last more than 20 minutes. If the sonata were a song without end, its place would certainly be among the instruments of the Devil's torture in hell.

Even the kiss…What lover could tolerate a kiss that never ended?

The poem also had to die to be perfect, to be beautiful, and for me to long for it after its end. Everything that is perfect asks to die. After death, the poem becomes silence—emptiness. Then something else will be born in its place: longing. Longing only flourishes in absence.

It is in longing that the gods are born—they exist so the lover that was lost can return, so that life may be like the phonograph record that can be played as many times as desired. Gods—I have no love of them in themselves. I love them only for that—their power to bring the embrace back so that it can repeat. The gods aren't divine. Re-encountering is divine.

Vinícius's voice was announcing the end. He shifts to speak in a lower voice.

Remaining, this daily dialogue with death,
this fascination for the moment to come, when,
touched, emotion comes to open the door like an
old lover (...)

And I, in my mind, automatically move ahead, reciting in silence the last verse:

...without knowing that she is my newest love.

So it was that, at the last moment, the unforeseeable happened: the phonograph needle jumped back—perhaps it found the poem so beautiful that it refused to be an accomplice to its end, did not accept its death, and there remained the dead voice of Vinícius repeating words without meaning:

78

"...without knowing it is my newest love..."
"...without knowing it is my newest love..."
"...without knowing it is my newest love..."

I got up from my place, went to the record player and consummated the murder. I gently pushed the arm with my finger and helped beauty die, helped it become perfect. It thanked me, said what it had to say: "...without knowing it was my newest love..." After that was the silence.

I thought about whether that was a parable of life, life as a work of art, a sonata, a poem, a dance. From the first moment, when the composer or the poet or the dancer prepares the work, the last moment is already in gestation. It's quite possible that the last line of the poem had been the first Vinícius wrote. Life is a fabric like the spider's web: it always begins at the end. When life begins at the end, it is always beautiful for being colored with the colors of twilight.

No, I don't believe that biological life should be preserved at any price.

"For every thing there is a season. A time to be born and a time to die." (Ecclesiastes 3:1-2)

Life is not a biological thing. Life is an aesthetic entity. When the possibility of feeling happiness before beauty dies, life dies, too, just as God intended even though

the paraphernalia of doctors continue to emit their beeps
and produce zig-zags on the video.

Life is like that song. It needs to die.

Death is the last chord, which says: It is complete.
Everything that is complete desires to die.

The Baptized

*M*y son Sérgio made a strange request. He asked me to plan a rite of baptismal for Mariana, my granddaughter. I told him that to go through with that rite, it was necessary to believe. I don't believe. For many years the words of priests and pastors have been empty for me, even though I continue to be fascinated by the beauty of the Christian symbols as long as they are contemplated in silence.

He didn't give up, and he argued: "But you did my wedding…" Yes. I remember how he "put in his order" for the ritual: "Dad, don't speak the words of religion! Just speak the words of poetry!" And that's the way it went. They were the words of "The Canticle of Canticles," an erotic poem from the Bible, which makes devout men and women blush. "Your two breasts are like two twins of a gazelle! (…) Your lips drip sweetness like honeycomb, and beneath your tongue milk and nectar are found." I enjoy thinking about the face the pope and bishops would make if they read those words. They were followed by words of Drummond, Vinícius, Adélia[8]—all ending not with the annoying "Marcha Nucial" ["Nuptial March"] but with Chico's "Valsinha,"[9] when the guests, young and old, grabbed their partners and set themselves to dancing. It was beautiful. When something is beautiful, we believe it easily.

So I remembered a passage from Alex Haley's *Roots* where he describes the name-giving ritual for newborns in an African tribe.

Omoro (the father) then walked out before all the assembled people of the village. Moving to his wife's side, he lifted up the infant and, as all watched, whispered three times into his son's ear the name he had chosen for him. It was the first time the name had ever been spoken as the child's name, for Omoro's people felt that each human being should be the first to know who he was. They beat drums. Omoro whispered the same name in his wife's ear, and she smiled with pleasure. Then it was the whole village's turn: "The name of the first son of Omoro and Binta Kinte is

---

8   Adélia Luzia Prado Freitas (b. 1935), Brazilian poet and writer who wrote about Catholicism and the body.

9   Chico Buarque de Hollands, (b. 1944), Brazilian composer, singer, dramatist, poet whose performances and recordings of the 1960-1970s criticized the military government and also celebrated romance, as the song "Valsinha" (Little Waltz) did.

Kunta!" After the full ritual, Omoro, carrying, little Kunta in his strong arms, walked to the edge of the village, lifted his baby with his face to the heavens, and said softly, *"Fend kiling dorong leh warrata ke iteh tee."* (Behold the only thing greater than yourself!)

This memory convinced me, and I tried to make up a name-giving ritual, since none that I knew of satisfied me.

I organized the space in the living room. I pushed the low coffee table toward the fireplace. At the head of the room I set an old bench. There Mariana would sit. To the side, two chairs—one for the father, the other for the mother. At the end of the table, a large candle. It's Mariana's candle, a candle that had been with her her whole life and which had to be lit on all her birthdays. To the side of the candle, two long, colored candles. And, scattered throughout the room, candles of all types and colors. At the edge of the table, beside Mariana's candle, a wooden dish with a bunch of grapes.

Once all the guests were assembled, the ritual began. This is what I said: "Mariana, we are here to tell you the story of your name. It all began in great darkness." The lights went out as we heard the sound of Jean-Pierre Rampal's flute.

"Thus was your mother's belly, a dark, calm and silent place. There you lived for nine months. Once that time had passed, you tired and said, "I want to see light!"

Your mother heard your plea and did as you wished. She gave you to the light.[10] You were born."

Mariana's mother and father then lit the big candle, which shined alone in the middle of the room.

"Just look what happened! Your light filled the room with joy. All the faces are smiling at you. And because of that joy, each one of them will also light their candle."

With that the godmother and godfather light the long, colored candles, and the others light, one by one, all of the candles around the room.

When the guests had arrived, I gave each one of them a little card where they were to write their deepest wish for Mariana. I continued:

"You brought such joy that each one of us wrote on a little card a good wish for you. So, take this basket. Go to each one and collect the good wishes that they have written. These little cards, you will keep them for the rest of your life…"

And Mariana went around with the basket and her big blue eyes, from person to person, being blessed by them all.

"Everyone has given you something good," I said after the cards were collected. "Now it is time for you to give everyone something good. You are as plump and sweet as a grape. That is the purpose of this bunch of grapes. This

84

---

10   The Portuguese expression for giving birth—dar à luz—translates directly as "give to the light."

is what you are going to do. Your godparents are going to make a little chair, and you, seated there, will give each one of them a piece of yourself, one sweet, plump grape.

And so, slowly, without knowing it, Mariana celebrated this unusual eucharist. "This sweet, plump grape is my body..."

When the eucharist was over, I said to Mariana:

"Now, coming to the end, each one of us is going to say your name. Pay good attention. The name is just one. But each one will say it with a different music. Because there are many different ways that you are loved."

And so, illuminated by the candles, each one of those present, looking deep into the girl's eyes, said, "Mariana," "Mariana," "Mariana," "Mariana."

Those who looked into Mariana's eyes could see that, as she heard her name being repeated, they filled with tears...

The Lake

J would like to invite you to go with me on an excursion. I will be the guide. An excursion is, more than anything, an experience with the senses: to see unseen sights, hear uncommon sounds, smell new essences, try strange foods, let your skin feel the sun, the cold, the wind. One doesn't go on an excursion to think. It isn't a matter of agreeing or disagreeing. It is simply a matter of experiencing with the body. Before leaving on an excursion, everyone should read, as a daily devotion, the poems of Alberto Caeiro[11]: "The world wasn't made to be thought but to be seen and to be agreed with."

I want to take you on a trip through my world, with the help of psychoanalysis. But for that, you need to unlearn it and to forget that which you know about it. To

---

11   A heteronym (that is, a fictional character created for the purpose of writing in a special style) used by Brazilian poet Fernando Pessoa.

lose theumemory. The memory doesn't let you see straight. Memory bothers the eyes.

I want you to forget that psychoanalysis is therapy. I want you to forget the words you normally use when discussion about psychoanalysis comes up: identification, transference, sexual repression, ego/id/superego, psychoanalysts, goddesses, honorariums. Psychoanalysis doesn't begin with these words. Psychoanalysis is, above all, a way of seeing the body. It is the most fascinating. It believes that inside the body there is a universe more fantastic, more incredible, more terrible, more mysterious than the universe outside. Science fiction takes us on trips to the ends of the universe. Psychoanalysis tries to do something similar—take us to the ends of our soul. The soul is larger than the astronomic universe. Psychoanalysis is a travel guide.

Many eyes see the body. Each eye sees it in a different way.

Medicine, for example, has many eyes. So many that the correct thing to say would be medicines, in the plural. The eyes of surgeons don't see the body the same way that general clinicians see it. If you went to a homeopath, he would ask you questions that a clinician never would. Chinese medicine, in turn, sees everything another way. When you opt for a type of doctor and turn down others, it's because you don't want your body to be seen by the eyes that you rejected. How curious: in the choice of a doctor, philosophy is present!

Religions, too, all of them, are different ways of seeing the body. The Christian religions see the body with eyes of guilt. The body, in the Christian world, finds itself always under the observation of The Big Eye that lets nothing slip by. In Taoism, there is no Big Eye. Taoism doesn't know what guilt is. For Taoism, the body is a little boat that goes sailing, taken away by the currents of a big river. For Christianity, the body isn't worth trust. It needs to be reprimanded. For Taoism, the body is wise and needs to be heard. In one, the debtor body, contested deeds. In the other, the sailing body, with no bills to pay.

How strange! It's certain that a solid, material, physical world exists. But we never see it. What we see are the worlds that reside inside our eyes. Don't believe it? Ask Kant.

Psychoanalysis is an eye with which we see a world different from the others. It wasn't psychoanalysis that discovered these worlds. It had already been seen by mystics, poets, and artists since time immemorial. They saw it and turned it sensible through painting, sculpture, music, poems, songs, cathedrals, cuisine, and literary works. The genius of psychoanalysis is that it discovered that the works of art are more than works of art: They are entries into the world of the soul. A dream—the prototype of all the works of art!

There's an enormous difference between the experience of art, on one side, which is essentially emotional, and the critique of art, on the other, which is essentially rational. To read in the newspaper today a critique of yesterday's concert in no way communicates the emotion that was had on hearing the concert yesterday. To read a critique of the exhibition of works by Dalí does not communicate the emotion that it was possible to have standing in front of his paintings. Besides the pure esthetic experience, there is the experience of thought: Dalí's body was in the same state as my body now in front of his painting... The experience of the beautiful is an experience of possession. Beauty becomes at one with the body, the body "turns into" a work of art. But the experience of criticism only touches my head. It isn't emotion. It's thought.

Psychoanalysis sees the body as a work of art. A work of art incarnate. Paraphrasing scripture, which says "The Word is made Flesh," I say, "Beauty is made Body."...But its relationship with this incarnate Beauty is the same relationship that exists between rational criticism and emotional experience. Psychoanalysis, as theory, is a rational exercise that investigates the "reasons," the human meaning that is found in the roots of this incarnate work of art. But the emotions are in another place.

I only know how to think by means of metaphors. The

metaphor is an image that is not a thing but which helps me see the thing. The mailman says to Neruda, "I am a ship beaten by the waves." Of course, he is not, literally, a ship. But whoever hears those words understands perfectly what he is saying. So, here comes my first metaphor for the world through which we are going to travel. Do you know how to dive? See if you can understand...

Before us, an immense lake. No breeze wrinkles its smooth surface. In it are reflected, inverted, the things of the outside world: willows, with their long branches, tall pine, the papyrus with its uncombed hair, white clouds sailing across the blue of the sky, the herons in their harmonious flight. Lake, mirror, where everything fits. Once in a while a fish jumps unexpectedly, quickly disappearing, leaving waves that disperse in a circle across the surface of the lake. A sudden rippling on the surface announces the passage of an invisible school of fish. Sometimes a simple fin cuts the water, betraying the presence of a big fish. And, near the banks, bubbles burst at the surface, coming from the dark depths. That's how the lake looks from outside. But if the observer is curious and unafraid, he can dive down. Thus he will see another world that the surface doesn't let be seen: tame, colored fish, aquatic plants, catfish and piranhas, rotted boats, the remains of wrecks, and every kind of shape that cannot be seen from the outside. The same lake: from outside, one thing; in the depths another.

The mystics, poets, and artists have long known that the body is a lake: the smooth surface reflects the outside world. But all you have to do is cross the mirror with a dive (don't be frightened by this image of crossing the mirror. Alice, from Lewis Carroll's book, did that, and the mirror didn't break. It melted. Give yourself the pleasure of reading *Alice in Wonderland* and *Through the Looking Glass*. Carroll was a wonderful guide to the world of psychoanalysis, even before it existed. Don't be fooled. These aren't books for children...) to arrive at a world that exists on the other side of the body, the side that outside can't see. Escher put both of these two worlds in a lovely drawing to which he gave the name *Air and Water*. Note the geese flying. They are black against a white background. Look what happens in the intervals as the eye descends. Shapes of fish begin to take form. Until, diving into the water, the depth is black. The fish appear as the geese disappear in intervals. Here a simple design is represented, the strange world that the mystics and artists see and which psychoanalysts try to understand. We ourselves are winged beings that fly in the luminous world, underwater beings that swim in a mysterious world.

"I'm Going Crazy..."

She arrived and, after a brief moment of indecision, said, "I think I'm going crazy…"

I remained silent, like a hunter waiting for the flight of the prey, because this is my profession. I am a hunter of words.

It was certain that some surprising change had occurred in her thoughts. Accustomed to tame, short-flight words that moved through her interior world every day, she must have been surprised at the sudden rising of another entity whose existence she had never suspected, hidden as it was in the shelter of the dense undergrowth that marks the edge of the obscurity of the soul. She had received the emissary of the unconscious—thoughts that she had never had, thoughts uncommon, unknown. She knew nothing of their origin nor of their destination. She had suddenly found herself without solid ground under her feet, floating over the mystery. That's what she had told me with her statement: "I think I'm going crazy..."

But I didn't know anything about the color, the shape, or the movements of this mysterious bird that was scaring her. So I remained quiet, waiting... I confess that I felt a shiver of pleasure. Caged birds are always banal and can be bought anywhere. I don't pay them any attention since the newspapers and daily chit-chat are full of them. But these wild birds who announce themselves with the name *crazy* are born of the unknown and take us flying to other worlds where we have never been.

So, she continued, explaining what had happened. "I am a practical, uncomplicated person. I like to cook. And I do it competently, automatically, without thinking. I cut the onions, the chives, the tomatoes, and I go on doing the things that must be done in the way I have always done them. These things and these acts were never worth my attention. While I cook, my thoughts are focused on the final dish and in the pleasure of eating with friends.

"But, last week, something strange happened. I picked up an onion like all the others, cut a ring as I always did, and was surprised. I sensed that I had never seen an onion. Was that possible? I've seen and cut hundreds of onions, and now it was as if I were seeing the onion for the first time! I looked at the rounded shape, felt the smoothness of its skin under my fingers, saw the rings, circular, perfect, one tucked into the next, the light fragmented in hundreds of shining points on its surface. My practical, unconscious thought was interrupted. I left the knife on the sink and was spellbound with the onion ring in my hand. I forgot about the dish I was preparing. At that moment, I didn't want to make any dish whatsoever for the delight of the mouth, because I had encountered another form of delight: the delight of the eyes. My eyes were eating the onion ring. And I sensed a pleasure I had never before sensed.

"For the first time in my life I saw that the onion is beautiful. If I were a painter, I would paint an onion. If I were a photographer, I would photograph an onion… My onion had left behind being just a creature from the produce section of the supermarket, at the mercy of knives and chewing jaws, and it seemed like an enchanted creature, resident of the world of beauty, beside jewels and works of art.

"When I awoke from the mystic trance, where I saw an onion ring as if it were a stained glass window in a Gothic cathedral, I became frightened. What strange thing must have happened to my eyes? What strange transformation must have been happening to me?

"If I told my friends what had happened, they would not understand. They would think that I was kidding. They would laugh. I had to remain silent about my experience.

Then I thought that I was going crazy. Because craziness must be this: that which you experience and have to keep quiet about. Because if you talk about it, others will not understand and will start to think that you've got a screw loose.

"But the worst is that what happened with the onion began to happen with everything. My eyes were no longer the same. There were possessed of a new psychedelic power. They saw what they'd always seen in a way they'd never seen. My paintings became different. My things became different. My plants became different. And most disturbing was the silly happiness that I sensed in everything. And I thought, if I keep feeling happy like this, all of my big plans will fall to the ground. If I feel joy at the smallest things, I'll stop struggling to accomplish big things…."

She was frightened of happiness. She was scared to sense that joy resided nearby. Seeing was enough. And I told her: "You aren't going crazy. You are becoming a poet…."

The poetic experience isn't the seeing of grand things that no one sees. It's seeing the absolutely banal that is in front of our noses…in a different light. When this happens, each daily thing is transformed into the entrance of an enchanted world. And you can begin a journey without leaving your place…. We find what we're looking for right before our eyes.You don't have to do anything.

You don't have to travel to distant places. Is there anything more useless than a trip when your eyes see everything in black and white? It also isn't necessary to accomplish great feats of struggle and work—because beauty can be found within reach. Blake said: "To see a world in a grain of sand and a heaven in a wild flower..." No, she wasn't going crazy. But I understood her fright. She had discovered the poetic. And the craziness of poetry is precisely in this: the understanding that it's enough for beauty to reside within the eyes so that the interior world is transfigured by them. Happiness is born from within the eye that has been touched by poetry.

In Praise of Uselessness

I thought I knew my garden. Because it was from my head that it grew. Each plant had a reason to be, a history. A memory. Looking at it was enough to awaken in me my passion for gardening: beds to water, weeds to pull, earth to turn over, limbs to prune, pests to kill. Pruning clippers and trowel in hand, I was utility from head to foot. Work was necessary.

Then I got sick (that surgery, a while ago…) and all of a sudden the garden became different. I began to see things I'd never seen. They'd always been there, right under my nose. But I, utilitarian and in a hurry, had never seen them nor smelled them nor felt them. Pain obliged me to be a way I normally wasn't. Pain, when it's there, hammering, is an awful thing. The world ends, and it ends up being that place where the pain drills through. But

97

there's another pain that stays off to the side, quiet, and says, "If you move, I will make you suffer…." Because this, my teacher, has taught me lessons, leaving me a little wiser. First, the lessons of humility, that feeling of absolute dependence that Schleiermacher identified as being the essence of religious sentiment. Before the mystery of life I can do nothing: I am alone. I am lonely.

Later, the virtue of patience. You have to know how to wait, because nature is slow. It still hasn't been reached by the insanity of rush. My plans for the day were forgotten, useless, with their lists of things to do and meetings to attend. With no pangs of conscience I felt the delightful feeling of not fulfilling a duty. To say *no* in a final and definitive way, leave the someone else speechless, with all the arguments that he had ready to convince me rendered futile. And, most important, it obliged me to do nothing. It taught me to live with, first, the affliction, and then with the delights of uselessness. I was unconcerned with my impotent, useless, dangling hands. Since I couldn't do anything, the only thing left was to contemplate, to receive.

There is a side of us that remains hidden, restrained, which only appears when we can't do anything. It's the receptive side, the pure pleasure of contemplation without trying to do anything. I just sat on the porch, watching. And the more I became at peace with my uselessness, the more the garden went into a striptease, showing me a nakedness

I had never seen.

First, the play of light on the leaves in the wind. The wind gusts, the leaves shake, forming configurations that never repeat. Since I couldn't do anything, the only thing left to do was be a spectator of the spectacle who says, "Very nice, encore, how beautiful!" And light, wind, and leaves thanked me and did a new dance.

I saw the shapes, the smooth and rugged trunks, thick and thin, solitary and branched, sunshade, lace, hearts, some dangling sad, other rising to the sky. Later, a curious dance from a hummingbird and a wasp, both seeking sugar water, disputing the same place. And the two of them became, for a moment, motionless in the air, one in front of the other, until the wasp, it seemed to me, recognized the hummingbird's rights and decided to withdraw.

I spotted the place where the waxbills had built a nest. I'd already heard their chirping several times, but I hadn't had time to see them disappear into the leaves of the bougainvilleas.

And the buzzards, wonderfully beautiful in the depths of the sky, not a single movement to disturb the peacefulness of their harmony with the wind. I also thought about the invisible movement of the vital fluids running through the plants, vegetal blood, silent manifestation of the mystery of life. And I accompanied the changes in the spirit of time. I heard the secrets of the mornings (joyous), midday (stopped) and afternoons (sad).

It was in the middle of this guiltless uselessness that I gave in to the luxury of books that for a long time had been awaiting me on the shelf. The to-do lists of important things (!) had obliged me to leave them for later. But now I was no longer something useful. I couldn't be used for anything. I enjoyed the supreme freedom of being absolutely useless and could hand myself over to the daydreams of thought without anyone demanding anything from me. I began with the heavy books. I got tired. I moved on to others, lighter, and finally I voraciously gave in to the supreme form of of uselessness: I began to read Agatha Christie. I forgot everything because all mysteries are the same and end the same way. But I didn't forget one page. The characters were discussing a painting of an old Chinese man absently involved in a game with strings. And someone commented, "You have to be very wise to be able to do nothing!" And I envied the old Chinese. I wasn't playing with strings, but the mystery books were still a spool of threads that needed to be untangled. I loved the old, unknown man, and I thought that maybe this is what we need to learn: to be less crazy and a little more wise, that there is a supreme form of happiness that we can enjoy only when we surrender to the delightful irresponsibility of uselessness. I liked the idea so much that I'm even going to write about it again.

Doing Nothing

The morning is the way I like it. Blue sky, cool breeze. Soon, still early, it invites me to do nothing. Take a walk—not for reasons of health but for pure pleasure. The pink *ipê* trees have blossomed before their time—have you noticed? And there's nothing more beautiful than the crown of an *ipê* tree against a blue sky. All anxious thoughts stop, and you become possessed by the pure thankfulness that life is so generous with beautiful things. There, under the *ipê*, there's nothing I have to do. There's nothing I should do. Any action on my part would be superfluous. Because how could I improve that which is perfect?

I remember my first lessons in philosophy, how I laughed when I read that, for Taoism, supreme happiness is that to which they give the name *Wu-Wei*—to do nothing. I thought they were crazy. Because in those days, I was an ethical being who judged that action was the most important thing. I still haven't learned the lessons of Paradise—that when we are before beauty, the only thing for us to do...is nothing, to enjoy the happiness that it offers us.

I wanted to ask the *ipê* trees the reason behind their ambivalence. Could it be, perchance, that they had no agenda? Because if they did, they would know that the blossoming of the *ipê* is scheduled only for the month of July. Anyone who pays attention to nature's seasons knows that. But, before I could ask my stupid question, I heard, inside myself, the answer they would have given me. They would have answered by citing the medieval mystic Angelus Silesius, who said that flowers have no why; they bloom because they bloom. I thought it would be good if we, too, were like plants, if our actions were a pure overflowing of vitality, a pure explosion of beauty that grew from within and could not longer be contained. Without why, for pure pleasure.

But now I look at the table, and a book with a green cover reminds me that I don't live in Paradise, that I don't have the right to live for pleasure. What everyone asks of me isn't that I blossom like the *ipê*s but that I fulfill my obligations—even though they take me a bit distant from my happiness. For obligation is this: that voice that shouts louder than my unborn flowers—my desires—and obliges me to do what I don't want. Because if I wanted to, it wouldn't need to shout. I would do it for pure pleasure. And if it shouts to obligate me to obey, it's because that which duty demands isn't that which the soul requests. Given that, look at the wisdom of two lines from Fernando Pessoa. First, the one where he says, "Ah, the lushness in the face of not fulfilling a duty!" Shameless, irresponsible, corruptor of youth, ought to be forced to drink hemlock like Socrates! It's none of that. It only tells the truth: we can be happy only when we are like the *ipês*, when we bloom because we bloom; when no one tells us what to do and what we are doing is only a child of pleasure. And the other verse, the one where he says that we are in the gap between what we desire and what others desire from us.

In my book with the green cover are written the desires of others. It is called an agenda. My own desires do not need reminders from anybody. They don't need to be written down. I know them by heart (yes, in my breast). By heart means in the heart.

That which is written in the heart does not need agendas because we don't forget it. Whatever the memory loves remains forever. If I need an agenda it's because it's not in my heart. It isn't my desire. It's the desire of someone else. My schedule tells me that I should leave my conversation with the *ipês* for later because there are duties to be done. And that I should remember the first lesson in morals administered to any child: first your duties, then your devotion; first the agenda, then the pleasure; first the desires of others, then your own desires. Isn't that the basis of all social life? A good, responsible person isn't the one who forgets his or her desires and obeys the desires of someone else—never minding that the other person lives inside himself or herself?

Ah! Many people have no soul. What they have in its place is an agenda. That's why they are incapable of understanding what I'm saying. In their agenda-souls there is no place for desire. In the place of the *ipê*s there is only an immense emptiness. There's an emptiness that is good: emptiness of hunger (which leaves a place for desire to eat); the emptiness of cupped hands (which makes a place where water can fall from the spigot); the emptiness of arms (which makes a place for a hug); the emptiness of longing (which makes a place for happiness to return).

But there's an emptiness that doesn't make a place for anything, a deserted-emptiness, a desert where demons live. And this emptiness, the tomb of desire, needs to be filled in some way. Because if it isn't, anxiety will come to live there.

Anxiety is a hole left by forgotten desire, the hole of a heart that no longer exists, a desperate shout asking for desire and the heart to come back so that the beauty of the crown of the *ipê* against the blue sky can be enjoyed. This emptiness is so terrible that various rituals have been created to exorcise the demons that live in it. One of them is my agenda—and the agenda of the whole world. When anxiety arrives, just reading the written instructions is enough. The hole is filled with commands and becomes an illusion that all is well. And is that why so much work gets done—from housewives sweeping homes to the stock market of businessmen? They are all the same. They all struggle against the same fear of emptiness.

And you, for whom life is furious work and restlessness—are you not weary of living? Are you not ripe for death's preaching? All of you for whom furious work is something dear—and also all that is fast, new and different—you find it too hard to bear yourselves; your industriousness is an escape, a desire to forget yourselves. You do not have the enough inside yourselves to wait—not even for idleness. (Nietzsche) That's why we turn on televisions—to fill the emptiness.

That's why we spend Sunday reading newspapers (even while our children are playing on the see-saw at the park)—to fill the emptiness. That's why we can't stand the idea of an idle weekend without doing somethin.g (And on Monday asking ourselves, "And next weekend, what are we going to do?") That's why even on the beach we fill ourselves with frenetic business—because we are afraid of the thoughts that might visit us in the calm of contemplating the sea, which never tires of doing the same thing.

The Taoists are right: supreme happiness is the *Wu-Wei* of doing nothing. Because only those who are at peace with life can receive the delights of contemplation and not forget their own desires.

"Whether It's Good or Bad..."

When I used to tell my daughter stories—she was still small—there was a question she always asked me: "Did this story really happen?" I had no way to respond.

If Peter Pan were an adult, as he is in *Hook*, I would say right away that everything was just a little white lie of no importance that I had made up so she would go to sleep soon and I could go back to taking care of the important things in the real world of money, politics, work, the household chores. I would tell her that the book that was important to me was the one I was really reading, my bedside book, was the agenda with the green cover. In its pages was written reality. But she was *still* very much a child. In time she would grow and learn to read the literature of the real that can be read in agendas. *Meanwhile* she could surrender to

107

the lying words of stories, just so sleep might come more quickly...

But I wasn't the grown-up Peter Pan, and what I had to say I would not say because I thought it was too complicated for her bedside table. What I would like to tell her and did not tell her is that *the stories I was telling never happened so that they can always happen.* Neverland is the Alwaysland that exists eternally inside us. That which has in fact happened—documented, photographed, proven by science and written in the name of history—happened outside of us and therefore will never happen again. This death is buried in the past, and there is no spell that can bring it back to life. But that which never happened, that which was only dreamed, is that which has always existed and always will, that which was never born and will never die, and every time it's told, it happens again...

If she had asked me a different way, if she had asked me if I believed in the story, ah!—I would answered easily: "But of course I believe!" Because I only believe what never happened, in dreams, because it is dreams that we are made of.

The story of Snow White never happened, but all of us are, always, a stepmother who sees herself sad before the mirror and sends the girl—who, too, is us—to be killed in the forest. The story of Hansel and Gretel never happened, but in every child there is the terrible fantasy of abandonment. The story of Romeo and Juliet never happened, but we want to hear it again because inside of us there is a dream of pure love, beautiful and immortal. And that's why I am incurably religious, because in the stories of religion, which never happened, the dreams and nightmares of the soul are reflected. I believe because I know they are a lie. If they were real, they would not interest me.

Stories are told like mirrors, so that we can discover ourselves. The orientals are great masters in this art, forgotten by occidentals because, like Peter Pan in the movie *Hook*, they grew up and went on to believe only in that which their agenda tells them, without noticing that, since it tells the truth, it lies.

I want to tell you the story that I have most told. It never happened. It always happens. A very rich man, upon his death, left his land to his sons. All of them got beautiful, fertile land, with the exception of the youngest, for whom was left a swamp that was useless for farming. His friends grew sad about that and visited him to lament the unfairness that had been done to him. But he said just one thing to them: "Whether it's good or bad, only the future can tell." In the next year, a terrible drought hit the country, and the land of his brothers was devastated. The springs dried up, the pastures grew parched, the cattle died. But the swamp of the youngest brother became a beautiful, fertile oasis. He became rich and bought a lovely white horse at a very high price. His friends organized a party because such a wonderful thing had happened. But they only heard one thing from him: "Whether it's good or bad, only the future can tell." The next day, his horse ran away, and his sadness was great. His friends came and lamented what had happened. But what the man said to them was the same words as always: "Whether it's good or bad, the future will tell." The next day, his son, without thinking, got on a wild horse. The horse bucked and threw him off. The boy broke a leg. The friends returned to lament the tragedy. "Whether it's good or bad, only the future will tell," the father repeated. A few days later, along came some soldiers of the king to take young men to war. All the boys had to go, minus the son with the broken leg. His friends celebrated and came to have a party. The father saw it all and said only one thing: "Whether it's good or bad, only the future can tell...."

Thus ends the story—with no end, just suspense. It could be continued indefinitely. And, as I tell it, it seems like the story of my life. My failures as well as my victories didn't last long. There is no professional or amorous victory that guarantees that life has finally resolved itself. No defeat could be a final condemnation. Victories are undone like sand castles touched by waves, and defeats turn into moments that proclaim a new beginning. As long as death does not touch us, since it alone is definitive, wisdom tell us that we always live at the mercy of unforeseeable accidents. "Whether it's good or bad, only the future can tell."

Adult Vision

*H*e himself told me, like a blind confession, later giving me permission to relate the miracle as long as I didn't reveal the saint. A doctor, he arrived at his office with his perfect eyes and his head full of thoughts. They were serious thoughts—surgeries, hospitals, and the illnesses that awaited him in the waiting room.

The first patient came in and tamely submitted to the medical palpations. When the consultation was over, the prescription written, as he was leaving he gave a word of praise: "Doctor, the orchids in your waiting room are so beautiful!"

My friend smiled with embarrassment, with the shame of saying that he hadn't noticed any orchid in the waiting room and therefore knew nothing of the beauty that the sick man had noted. He was ashamed to reveal his blindness. The second patient came in. After the consultation, unable to contain what he felt, the patient said, "The orchids in your waiting room are wonderful, doctor!" Again he smiled wanly, unable to say anything about the orchids he hadn't seen.

In came the third patient, and the same thing happened the same way. So the doctor excused himself, left the room and went to see the orchids that the gardener had placed in the waiting room. They were, in fact, beautiful. But then came the aggravating part. The patient, not satisfied with the humiliation imposed on the blind doctor, noted that on the previous week, the tree in the office, planted in an immense vase in the corner, wasn't the same that had been there on that day. But the blind doctor with the perfect eyes hadn't noticed the presence of the tree on that day or on the previous week...

Ah! You are surprised that such blindness can exist! But I guarantee you that that's the way the eyes of adults work in general.

There go the mother and child, down the path, the child dragged by the arm. Holding onto the arm is more efficient than holding onto the hand. The two go down the same path, but they don't go down the same path. Blake said that the tree that the fool sees isn't the same tree the wise one sees. So I say that the path that the mother walks

113

isn't the same path that the child walks.

The eyes of the child go like butterflies, jumping from thing to thing, up and down, off to the sides, landing on the cocoon of a cicada on the trunk of a tree, he wants to stop to get it, but his mother gives him a yank, the kid continues, and not far ahead he sees the curious spectacle of two dogs in a strange game, one playing horsey on the other, wants his mother to see, sure she'll enjoy it, but instead of laughing, she gets mad and gives a stronger yank, so then the kid sees a blue fly floating inexplicably in the air, such a strange thing, what a beautiful color, he tries to catch the fly, but it gets away, and his eyes then hit on an almond on the ground, the kid turns into a soccer player, goes kicking the almond, later it's the dried seed pod of a flamboyant tree asking to be shaken…and so goes the kid, looking for everything that lives along all the paths, how much fun it is to walk, it's a shame his mother doesn't know how to walk because she doesn't have eyes that know how to play, she's in a big rush, needs to get there, there are urgent things, her thoughts are on the obligations of a housewife, that's why she keeps angrily shoving her kid, if only she'd look and play with toys that reside along the path, she wouldn't need psychoanalysis…

The mother walks at a resolute pace, an adult pace of one who knows what she wants, looking ahead and to the ground. Looking at the ground she looks for stones in the path, not for the love of Drummond but to not stumble, and she is also watching out for puddles, not because she has been moved by Escher's beautiful engraving called *Puddle*, a pool of dirty water reflecting blue sky and green pine branches, but because she is watching out for puddles so she doesn't dirty her shoes. Adults don't see Drummond's stone and Escher's dirty puddle, only children and artists see them. The mother wasn't born that way. She was once little, her eyes just like those of the son she is now dragging along. They were vagabond eyes, playful eyes that looked at things to be played with. And that's why little babies have the strange custom of putting everything they see into their mouths, telling us that everything is delicious, everything is to be eaten, everything is to be put inside the body. What the eyes desire, really, is to eat what they see. Neruda said so, confessing to be able to eat mountains and drink seas. Eyes are born playful and vagabond—they look for the pure pleasure of looking, something that now and then still appears in adults in the pleasure of seeing art. But then the mother got educated along a path like this one, her mother, too, dragging her by the arm, and when she tripped over a stone or stepped in a puddle because her eyes were vagabonding around with blue flies and shameless dogs, her mother was tugging her and saying, "Watch where you're going, girl! Watch where you're going!" That's how adult eyes are. Eyes aren't toys, they're path-breakers. They open paths in the direction that should be gone. That's how my friend's eyes. She used them to cut onions without cutting her finger until, one day, she saw what resided inside her eyes and she saw the wonderful beauty of translucent stained glass that resides in the rings of all onions, and she was so shocked by what she saw that she thought she was going crazy...Poor adults! They rip out their childish, playful vagabond eyes and replace them with work-tool eyes, path-breakers. That's how my doctor friend's eyes were. They saw neither the orchids nor the tree that were inside his office. His eyes were slaves of duty. And he didn't notice that the things around him were toys that ask his eyes, "Play with me! It's so much fun! If you play with me, I'll be happy, and you will be happy...."

The Name

*M*y friend Amilcar Herrera is a wise man. This is surprising given that he is a scientist. The fact is, science and wisdom are very different things. Science is knowledge of the world. Wisdom is knowledge of life. The exuberance of scientific knowledge frequently goes alongside a total penury of wisdom. Scientific knowledge can be like the pest known as mistletoe, a terrible parasite that lodges on the trunks of trees. As it grows, the tree dies. I am tired of seeing Ph.D. fools.

One of the characteristics of words of wisdom is that they surprise us. Guimarães Rosa cites an intriguing aphorism that says, "That which I am going to know without knowing I already knew." And that's exactly what the wise do. They already knew. But they didn't know. They knew without words. The wise open the mouth and we are

117

surprised to hear something said that was already residing dormant in the silence of the body.

Amilcar spoke, and I was surprised. He said:

Rubem, I have a dream. I dream that someday I am going to wake up and will have forgotten my name. I'll ask myself, Who am I? I won't know how to answer. I'll have no memory of my name. The worst thing is when you forget your name but other people continue to remember who you are. The psychiatrists say we have an attack of amnesia. And they try to cure us, make us remember the name so we can know who we are. The name is a cage where what we are lives. They pronounce us cured when our being appears again in the cage. It would be good if others also forgot our name. Then they would have forgotten the memory of the cage that imprisoned our being. And our being would transform itself into a bird that flew free through spaces where it had never flown. A name is a prison.

118

I must confess that these were not precisely Amilcar's words. We had that conversation a long time ago. But those were the associations that his statement provoked in me. That's what he said, the likes of which I had never thought. It was, for me, a revelation. I saw, all of a sudden, what I had never seen. That was it. Names are cages. In them the things we've done are stored. There are even resumés, cages of paper and words where, under our name, we put the things we have done. And there, based on what we have done, other people and we ourselves imagine that which can be expected of us.

C.S. Peirce, a respectable logician, in his essay on "How to Make our Ideas Clear," offers us this formula to help us have clarity about the nature of any object. "Consider what practical effects we imagine that this object could have. Then, the sum of these effects is what our concept of this object is." For example, the object "hen"—what practical effects are called up by this name in our thoughts? Answer: clucking, nest, eggs, droppings, scratching the ground, blood sauce, cracked corn, etc. These practical effects, summed up, are that which, in my head, are contained in the name "hen." So I ask myself, "How was it that I came to associate these practical effects with the name *hen*"? Answer: "By my past experience with this clucking chicken entity." So the name is a bag where the past experience can be held. And based on this experience we can know what to conclude about the future. No one will imagine that a hen is going to sing like a goldfinch or lay blue eggs or that it will make nests like those of hummingbirds. A hen is a hen, forever. It's in the name.

What's said of the hen applies to all. To people, too.

When my name is pronounced, I am immediately informed of what I have done in the past. And, on being informed, by the spellbinding sound of my name, of that which I have done in the past, I am also informed of my being and of that which is expected of me in the future. Thus the name obliges me to be the way that I am expected. The name contains the agenda of my being.

Amilcar knew things. I imagine that that confession— "I dream that someday I will wake up and I will have forgotten my name..."—was born of pain, the same pain that Álvaro de Campos put into a verse: "I am the interval between what I desire to be and what others have made me." He wakes up in the morning with I don't know what desire—there are people whose presence at a market or in a church is unthinkable; it just doesn't fit; the handsome surgeon in white is unthinkable in a market, buying onions, in shorts and sandals, and we also can't imagine a professed atheist professor of economy calling out to St. Barbara in the middle of a lightning storm (on invocations to St. Barbara, it's worth reading Alberto Caeiro). So I imagine Amilcar woke up with some strange desire unforeseen in his name, a desire he'd never had, or that he'd always had but whose recognition had always been prohibited by his name. But along came the interdiction: "This act is not permitted for the name Amilcar Herrera. This action is not foreseen in Amilcar Herrera's agenda."

So I understood the curious custom of a primitive people who always gave two names to people. The first is the same as ours, announced, spoken, written, known. People shout the name and people respond. The other name only the person himself or herself knows. The first name is a false name, only for practical effects, a socially necessary lie. The other name, secret, is the place where my true being resides, which is much different from the other. So through this trick, everybody knows that no one is imprisoned in a cage of sounds, that a person cannot be demanded to be, in the future, that which was kept in the bag of the name in the past. Each person has a secret inside, a mystery. Every little dappled donkey has, inside, a wild horse. Every pet duck has, inside, a wild goose. Every old man has, inside, a child who wants to play.

I think this is what Amilcar was saying:

If I write my name and if others don't demand that I continue to be what I was, then something new can be born of the old thing: a spring in the desert. In the end, this is the supreme promise of the evangelicals: that the old will be born again and will turn into children.

The Thousand and One Nights

J am surrendering myself to the lazy pleasure of rereading *The Thousand and One Nights*. The enchantment starts with the title, which, in the words of Jorge Luis Borges, is one of the most beautiful in the world. According to him, its particular beauty is owed to the fact that the word *thousand* is, for us, almost synonymous with infinity. "To talk about a thousand nights is to talk about infinite nights (...). To say *a thousand and one nights* is to go beyond infinity."

The Thousand and One Nights is the story of a

love—a love that never ends. Don't the immortal verses of Vinicius de Morães have room there (words so beautiful that the Devil himself used them in his argument with the Creator): "It may not be immortal, since it is a flame, but while it lasts, it's infinite." These are the words of someone who has felt the waft of wind inside that will soon blow that candle out—a declaration of love that foretells a parting.

But that's what those who love cannot accept. Even those for whom the flame has gone out dream of hearing from someone, someday, the words that Heine wrote to a woman: "I will love you eternally and even afterward." The flame must never go out, even though the candle goes on consuming itself. The art of loving is the art of not letting the flame go out. You can't let the light sleep. You have to hasten to awaken it (Bachelard). And, a curious thing, the same flame that the wind so impetuously blows out returns to be lit again by the caress of a soft breath...

The Thousand and One Nights is a story of the struggle between the impetuous wind and the soft breath. It reveals the secret of love that never goes out.

A sultan, finding himself betrayed by the wife he loved madly, made a cruel decision. He couldn't live without the love of a woman. But he also couldn't stand the possibility of betrayal. So he decided that he would marry the most beautiful girls in all his lands. But, after the first night of love, he would have them beheaded. So each day love would be renewed in all the vigor of reckless fire, with no breath of infidelity to blow it out. The word spread across the kingdom that terrible things were happening in the royal palace. The young women were disappearing right after the nuptial night. Scheherazade, daughter of the vizier

123

[who procured the young women] went to her father and told him her shocking decision: She wanted to become the sultan's wife. Her father, desperate, revealed to her the sad destiny that awaited her, since it was he himself who took care of the executions. But the young woman would not be dissuaded.

The way the story describes young Scheherazade is revealing. Almost nothing is said of her beauty. The story is silent on her erotic virtuosity. But it says that she read books of all kinds, that she had memorized a large number of poems and stories, that she knew by heart the popular proverbs and the dictums of philosophers.

And Scheherazade married the sultan. Performing the acts of physical love that took place on the nuptial nights, when the fire of carnal love had drained the body of her husband, when all that was left was to await the light of day so that the young woman could be sacrificed, she began to talk. She told stories. Her words penetrated the sultan's vaginal ears. Softly, like music. The ear is feminine, a space that waits and receives, that allows itself to be penetrated. Speech is masculine, something that grows and penetrates the spaces of the soul. According to an ancient tradition, that's how the human god was conceived—by the poetic breath of the divine Word penetrating the enchanted and receptive ears of a Virgin.

The body is a wonderful place of delights. But

Scheherazade knew that all love built on the delights of the body has a short life. The flame goes out as soon as the body has emptied itself of its fire. Its sad fate is to be decapitated in the morning. In that it's a flame, it isn't eternal. So, when the flames of the body have gone out, Scheherazade blew softly. She spoke. She eroticized the sultan's dormant emptiness. She awakened the magical world of fantasy. Each story contained another inside itself, infinitely. There is no orgasm that puts an end to desire. And she looked beautiful to him as no other. Because a person is beautiful not for her beauty but for our beauty reflected in her...

As the story goes, the sultan, enchanted by Scheherazade's stories, kept putting off the execution for a thousand and one nights—eternity and one day more.

This isn't one love story among others. To the contrary, it is the story of the birth and life of love. Love lives on this subtle thread of conversation, swinging between the mouth and the ear. Sonia Braga, at the end of the documentary celebrating sixty years of Tom Jobim, said that Tom was a man whom all women would like to have. And she explained: "Because he is masculine and feminine at the same time...." The secret of love is an androgyne. Aall of us, men and women, are male and female at the same time. All you have to do is listen. Take in. Let the other come inside us. Listen in silence. Without expelling the other with argument or contradiction. Nothing is more fatal to love than a quick answer, a saber that decapitates. There are very old people whose ears are still virgins. They were never penetrated. And it's necessary to know how to speak. Some speech is rape. The only one who know how to speak are those who know how to make silence and how to listen—above all, those who dedicate themselves to the difficult art of guessing: guessing the dormant worlds that reside in the spaces of others.

The Thousand and One Nights is a story of each one of us. In each of us there lives a sultan. In each of us there lives a Scheherazade. Those who are dedicated to the subtle and delicious art of making love with the mouth and the ear (those sexual organs that I've never seen mentioned in books on sex education...) can be the hope that the mornings will never end with the wind that blows out the candle but with the breath that relights it.

The Red Blazer

Buy jeans, sneakers, and a tee.
And if you have enough courage,
by a red blazer...

J love Tomiko. It's an old, gentle love. I love Tomiko as one loves an ikebana, a bonsai, a *baikai*. She is of pure simplicity and of Nipponese purity. Because Tomiko, on the same day that I enrolled in the age of sex, that is, when I became sex/age/narian, someone called me by phone with some surprising information which immediately turned into a challenge. I was told that in Japan, when a man turns 60, he buys a red blazer. Before that age he has no right to that color—attributable to the gods. Only at the age of 60 is this freedom granted him. Whoever has permission to use red has permission for everything.

Around here it's just the opposite. The older we get, the more colors are supposed to become sadder and more subdued. This custom, I believe, has something to do with

127

our idea that the aged have one foot in the grave and that it's good to be leaving the reds, blues, and yellows behind as we assume the gravity of one who is about to meet God, the same who created the rainbow and its seven colors but who never dressed in yellow with purple fringes.

The way that society chose for the elderly is a *preparatio mortis*. There's no other reason why in certain regions of the Iberian peninsula old women and widows (it's a general custom for men to die first) wear black from head to toe, a lugubrious imitation of the vestments of priests and buzzards, specialists in cadavers. With their black clothes they are declaring, "I have left life! I have abandoned love! May no man dare to desire me!"

The custom arrived at us in attenuated form, but it arrived. Not long in the past, modesty and respect required married women, after the age of 50, to wear tube dresses down to the ankles, closed at the neck, long sleeves, blue with little white balls, and hair in a bun. Men also, out of respect, had to always go around in a suit jacket, a vest, and a tie, obligatorily of somber color. A red blazer was only for Carnaval parties and the insane asylum.

But I decided to buy a red blazer. I am pleased to see the shocked faces of other people. I decided, but I didn't follow through. I lacked the courage. Anyway, we went traveling—my wife and I and another couple, Jether and Lucília. Wonderful people. Suffice it to say we were capable of traveling for a whole month in the same car, never getting annoyed with each other. We even agreed on the time to get up. Jether was 70 years old. But to see him, you wouldn't believe it. Elegant, black hair, smooth skin, tackles anything, climbs hills, descends hills, goes into the back woods, bathes under waterfalls, dives into lakes of freezing water—and his wife doesn't fall behind. Jether and Lucília are a couple of teenagers. So we went to Berlin, stayed at the house of their son, Luiz, who'd been living there for 20 years. One lovely morning, Luiz showed up for breakfast in a fancy blazer the color of bordeaux. The old resolution lit up in me again. Luiz told me that he'd bought that blazer at a used clothing store. We finished our coffee and went after the red blazer. I found a handsome one, very new, very cheap. The shame: it was a size small for me. It was a tight fit. But it was perfect for Jether. I soon became envious: he with a blazer, me with no blazer. But then came the disappointment. He didn't buy the red blazer even though he thought wine color nice. He claimed it didn't go well with his age. It wouldn't be right. Others would think it strange.

129

The others. Society has a special place for old people. A long time ago, they said of a "good negro" that "he knows his place." Something like that can be said of the good oldster: "He knows his role"—the role that the younger generations assign to him. The young accuse their old parents of being square. With that they want to say that their parents don't understand their values, their aesthetic tastes, their sexual customs, their songs. So it's useless to talk with them.

Now imagine that the father or the mother of some youngster all of a sudden, as a result of a stroke, changed his or her mind and started to like rock, started hanging out at bars, changed their old clothes for jeans and young colors and bought a convertible—what would happen? Would the son be happy that his father or mother had stopped being square? No way. He'd be smothered in shame.

In real life, it's right for them to be square. The old person who isn't square is, in reality, a cause of embarrassment and shame. I am reading again Simone de Beauvoir's *The Coming of Age*. Terrible. Society has a beautiful ideal for the elderly: white hair, rich in experience, patient, wise, tolerant, forgiving. Society assigns them the virtues of angelic beings, very different from normal human beings. The elderly have ceased to have the rights common to the young and adults. Simone says: "If the elderly presented the same desires, the same feelings, and the same demands as the young, the world would look on them with revulsion. In them, love and jealousy seem revolting and absurd, sexuality repulsive, violence ridiculous."

But the one who told the truth about the aged was Marcel Proust. "An old person is only an adolescent who has lived too long." In the body of an old man lives a teenager. Society does everything it can to free itself from this inconvenient intruder. It hides him behind a smiling mask, secretly kills him and buries him in a tomb of hypocrisy. But the teenager arises from death on the third day.

So today, as an Easter celebration, I invite you who are classified as old to release the teenager who lives in your body. Do something unusual, something prohibited that will horrify the young. Take your wife to a motel. Buy the underwear of a kid or some sexy panties with lace. Go to a bar, put yourself among the girls. Cancel your trip to Fátima. Go to the Chapada Diamantina or go swim in Bonito. Buy some jeans, sneakers, a t-shirt. And, if you have enough courage, buy a red blazer. I bought one, and I'm going to wear it. Later I found out that Jether didn't buy it only to not raise suspicions. His inner teen is always loose. Jesus Christ has been reborn from the dead. Hallelujah!

The Gardener and the Fräulein

Just a boy from far away, he'd seen the fishermen in boats carried by the wind. He thought that the sea had no end. He thought that the fishermen were happy because they didn't need to plant fish to harvest later. The sea was generous. The sea itself planted the fish that the fishermen only had to harvest with their nets. He envied the fishermen. He was a son of farmers. He had to plant what he harvested. Different from the sea, the land had an end. Every piece of land, the smallest and most insignificant bits, had all been cultivated. The fishermen, if they wanted more, all they had to do was sail off into the sea. But the farmers couldn't want more. The land had come to an end. Whoever wanted more land to plant would have to leave the known earth and go in search of new lands, beyond the endless sea.

He'd heard the oldest men talking about that—a country on the other side of the sea, so far away that there it was night when in his country it was day, a country of people with different faces, different food, different language, different religion, different customs. Everything was different. Minus one thing: the land was the same, and its secrets he already knew.

And that's how the day came that he, a teenager, his brother and his parents got on a ship that would take them to that country—what was its name again? Buragiro...that's how they, the Japanese, said the name *Brazil*...

In Brazil, Hiroshi Okumura—that was his name— managed to find work at the house of a family of Germans. It was a wealthy family, a house with lots of kids. Hiroshi spoke neither Portuguese nor German. But that didn't matter. His work was to care for the flower and vegetable gardens. And the language of the land and the plants he knew very well. The proof of this was in the bushes artistically trimmed according to the millennial inspiration of the bonsai, the plots bursting with flowers, the lush vegetables. And that's how, in his silent and faithful competence as a gardener, that his employers came to love him.

133

But no one came anywhere near suspecting the dreams that were in the gardener's soul. Those who don't know anything think gardeners just dream about earth, water, and plants. But gardeners also have dreams of love.

Gardens without love are beautiful and sad. But, when love bloom, the garden is happy and fragrant. And that was the secret that resided in the soul of the Japanese gardener. He loved a woman, a little German woman, a servant like him. Everyone called her *fräulein*. She had hair the color of copper like he'd never seen in his country, skin salted with freckles, blue eyes, and a shy smile on her succulent mouth that turned into laughter when she was apart from her employers. She was the one who brought him a plate of food, always with that smile...

And he dreamed. He dreamed that his hands caressed her hair and her face. He dreamed his arms embraced her and her arms embraced him. He dreamed that his mouth and his tongue drank love from that fleshy mouth. And his imagination did what imagination does with people in love. It imagined a ritual of love as delicate as that of a tea ceremony, undressing the *Fräulein* and kissing her skin... The imagination of a Japanese gardener in love is like the imagination of everyone in love...

But it was only a dream. He looked at his stocky body and simple clothes, his hands dirty with earth, his fingers as rough as stone. The *Fräulein* belonged to a world far from his gardener's world.

Once in a while he offered her a flower when she brought him food. She smiled that beautiful childlike smile, thanked him, and then skipped back to the house with the flower in her hand. But there were times she took the flower and brought it to her freckled nose to smell its perfume. The petals of the flower brushed her lips. And his gardener's body quivered, imagining that his mouth was touching her lips.

But his love never left fantasy.

No one ever knew. The years passed. He grew old. The *Fräulein* also aged. But his love did not diminish. For him, it was as if the years had not passed. She as still the little freckled girl. Unsatisfied love does not see the passage of time. It is eternal.

Finally the inevitable moment arrived. Getting old, he could no longer do his job. His employers, who loved him deeply, thought the best thing might be to let him spend his last years in a home for elderly Japanese, a large area of 50 acres, well planted, with birds, flowers, and a lake with carp and tilapias. He agreed. He visited the home, but, for unknown reasons, he didn't want to live there. He thought it better to live with relatives in a rural town. But the fact is, old people are always a bother in the life of younger people. They are, at best, tolerated. And his old age filled him with sadness.

135

One day, motivated by health, he decided to visit the house where he had spent his whole life and where the *Fräulein* lived. But there they told him that she had been put in a home for elderly Germans. She was very ill. So he went to visit her. He found her in a bed, very weak, unable to walk.

And then he did something crazy, something that only someone in love can do. He decided to stay with her. He slept by her side, on the floor. He cared for her as one would care for a child. (I am moved to think of the sensibility of the directors of that home who allowed this arrangement, which was unforeseen by the rules.)

The *Fräulein* was very weak. She couldn't even chew her food. She couldn't eat. Then, an unbelievable act of love took place. The gardener chewed food, then placed in in the mouth of, now, "his" *Fräulein*. The directors of the home, I believe motivated by love, made like they didn't see.

No one ever saw, no one ever told me. I imagined it. I imagined that when they were alone, with no one to see them, the gardener laid his lips on the *Fräulein's* lips, and that's how he fed her....That's how lovers do it, lips together, playing at passing a grape from one mouth to the other...

And then, at the end of life, the gardener kissed his *Fräulein* as he had never imagined kissing.... Love takes place in unexpected ways.

This is a true story. It happened. It was told to me by Tomiko, a friend who works with the elderly (the same who advised me to buy a red blazer). She knew the gardener personally.

On my little place in the country I plant trees for friends who have died. So I'm going to plant a cherry tree and a red rose, one beside the other: the Japanese gardener and his *Fräulein*.

Friendly Loneliness

*N*ight fell, work ended, and it was time to go home. Home sweet home? But the house was dark, the television off, everything silent. No one to open the door, no one waiting. You are alone. The sadness of loneliness comes... What you most desire is to not be in solitude.

But let me tell you something. Your sadness doesn't come from solitude. It comes from the fantasies that arise from solitude. I remember a young man who loved solitude— to be alone, to read, to listen to music... So on Saturdays, he prepared for a night of contented solitude. But all he had to do was sit down for the fantasies to arise. Scenes. On one side, friends at jovial parties, in the middle of a gabfest, the laughter, the beer. Then the scene changes. Him alone in that room. Certainly no one was remembering him. At that happy party, who would remember him? And then sadness entered, and he could no longer enjoy his friend solitude. The cure was to go out, meet up with a bunch of people to find the happiness of that party. He dressed up, went out to the party... But at the party he noticed that real parties aren't like the imagined parties. It wasn't a get together. It was an impossibility of sharing his solitude. The night was lost.

Let me make a suggestion. Read the book *The Flame of a Candle* by Bachelard. It's one of the most lonesome and beautiful books I have ever read. The flame of a candle, as opposed to the lights of electric lights, is always solitary. The flame of a candle creates around itself a circle of gentle light that gets lost in the shadows. Bachelard meditates before the flame of a solitary candle. Around him, shadows and silence. No idiot gabfest or easy laughter to disturb the truth of his soul. Reading Bachelard's solitary book, I find communion. I always find communion when I read. The great communions don't happen in the middle of laughter at a party. They happen, paradoxically, in the absence of others. It is precisely in the absence that proximity is greater. Bachelard, absent: I embraced him, thankful that he understood me so well. As he observes, "It seems that there are in us shadowy stories that tolerate only flickering light. A sensitive heart likes fragile values." Bachelard's solitary candle illuminated by my shadowy corners, got me to see things that hid when other people were around. And he asked me a question which I judge to be fundamental and which I propose to you as a reason to meditate: "How does your solitude behave?" My solitude? Is there a solitude that is mine, different from the "solitudes" of others? Does solitude behave? If my solitude behaves, it isn't just a crude, dead reality. It has life.

Among the many deep things that Sartre said, this is the one I love the most: "It doesn't matter what they do to you. What matters is what you do with what they have done to you." Stop. Read that again. And think. You lament the evil that life has been doing to you, the solitude. If Sartre is right, this evil could be the place where you are going to plant your garden.

How does your solitude behave? Or maybe, turning the question around: How do you behave with your solitude? What are you doing with your solitude? When you lament it, you are saying that you want to free yourself from it, that it is a suffering, a sickness, an enemy... Learn this: Things are the names that we give them. If I call my solitude an enemy, it will be my enemy. But is it possible to call it a friend? Drummond thinks so:

> *For a long time I have believed*
> *that absence is a lack.*
> *And, ignorant, I lamented the lack.*
> *Today I don't lament it.*
> *There is no lacking in absence.*

Absence is a being within me.
I feel it, clear, so gripped,
snuggled in my arms, that I laugh and dance
and make up joyous exclamations,
because absence, this assimilated absence,
no one can steal from me anymore!

Nietzsche also had solitude as his companion. Alone, ill, he had migraines that lasted three days and left him blind. He took his happiness in long walks through the mountains, from music and from a few books that he loved. Three wonderful companions! I often see people who walk for reasons of health. Unable to walk alone, they go in pairs and groups. And they talk and talk, without seeing the wonderful world that encircles them. They talk because they can't stand to walk alone. And that's how they miss the joy of walking, which is the joy of being in communion with nature. They don't see the trees or the flowers or the clouds or feel the wind. Such a sad swap! They exchange the voices of silence for the vulgar talkathon. If they were at one with nature, in silence, their solitude would make it possible for them to hear what nature has to say. The state of togetherness doesn't mean communion. The state of togetherness is often a terrible form of solitude, a trick to avoid contact with us ourselves. Sartre arrived at the point of saying, "Hell is other people." Who knows, maybe we'll talk about that some other day... But, returning to

Nietzsche, here's what he wrote about his solitude.

> *O solitude! My home, solitude!…Your voice—it speaks to me with tenderness and happiness!*
>
> *We don't talk, we don't complain, and often we walk together through open doors.*
>
> *For wherever you are, there things are open and shining. And even the hours walk fleet-footed.*
>
> *There the words and the times/poems of the whole being open before me. There the whole being desires to turn into words, and all change seeks to learn from me how to talk.*

And Vinicius? You remember his poem "The Construction Worker." The construction worker lived in the amid many people, working, talking. And while working and talking, he didn't see anything, didn't understand anything. but it happens that…

(…) one day, at the table, cutting bread, the worker was taken with a sudden emotion as he realized, amazed, that everything in that house—bottle, plate, machete— it was he who had made them, he, a humble worker, a construction worker. (…) Ah! Men of thought, you will never know how much that humble worker knew at that moment! In that empty house that he himself had raised up, a new world was born, a world he had never suspected. The worker, overcome with emotion, looked at his own hand, his rough worker's hand, and, looking at it closely, for a second had the impression that nothing in the world had ever been so beautiful. It was inside the comprehension of that solitary instant that, like his constructions, the worker also grew. (...) And the worker reaches a new dimension— the dimension of poetry.

Ranier Maria Rilke, one of the most dense and solitary poets that I know of, said the following: "Works of art are from an infinite loneliness." It is in solitude that they are created. It was in the empty house, in a solitary moment, that the worker saw the world for the first time and became a poet. And I also remember Cecília Meireles, so beautifully described by Drummond:

> (...) She didn't seem to me to be an unquestionably real creature; and the more I assess the positive traits of her presence among us, marked by gestures of courtesy and sociability, the more I was left with the impression that she wasn't where we saw her... distance, exile, and travel showed through her benevolent smile. Where did the real Cecília wander...?

Yes, there she was, delightfully among others, participating in the game of gregarious relationships that delightfulness obliged her to play. But the real Cecília was far, very far away, in a place where she was irremediably alone.

The first philosopher that I read, the Dane Sören Kierkegaard, a solitary man who has kept me company to this very dayy, observed that the beginning of human unhappiness is found in comparison. I experienced this with my own flesh. It was when I, a hick of a kid in a little town in the backlands of Minas Gerais, moved to Rio de Janeiro, that I knew unhappiness. I compared myself with them— the smart, well spoken, rich *cariocas*—residents of Rio. I was different. I had a ridiculous accent, and I stammered in shame. I was poor. Among them I was no more than an ugly duckling that others enjoyed pecking. I was never invited to go to any of their homes. I never invited any of them to come to mine. I didn't dare. So I knew loneliness. I suffered a lot. I never dared to share this suffering with my parents. It would be useless. They wouldn't understand. And even if they understood, they wouldn't be able to do anything. So, I had to suffer my loneliness alone, twice. What I am today formed inside that loneliness. Treks through the desert made me strong. I learned to take care of myself. And I learned to look for the things that, to me, alone, made sense. Like, for example, classical music, the beauty that makes my loneliness happy.

Your unhappiness with loneliness: Don't you derive part of it from comparisons? You compare the scene of yourself, alone, in the empty house, with the (fantasized) scene of other people at parties full of laughter. This comparison is destructive because it is born from envy. You suffer the real pain of loneliness because loneliness hurts. It hurts with a pain from which beauty can be born. But don't suffer the pain of comparison. It isn't real pain.

Love Letters

I read and re-read a poem by Álvaro de Campos. I don't know whether I should believe it or doubt it. If I believe, I doubt. I doubt because I believe. Because it was he himself who said—or better, his other person, Fernando Pessoa—that he was a pretender. "All love letters are ridiculous. They wouldn't be love letters if they weren't ridiculous…"

In my office I have a reproduction of one of the most delightful paintings that I know of. *Woman in Blue Reading a Letter*, by Johannes Vermeer (1632-1675). A woman, standing, reads a letter. Her face is lit by the light of a window. Her eyes read what is written on that piece of paper that her hands hold, her mouth slightly open, almost in a smile. She's so absorbed that she doesn't even notice the chair at her side. She reads on foot. I think I'm capable of reconstructing the moments that preceded the one that the painter froze. Knocks at the door interrupt the household routine. She opens the door, and there's the mailman with a letter in his hand. By simply reading her name on the envelope, she knows who sent it. She takes the letter, and with that gesture she touches a distant hand. That's why love letters are written. Not to give news, not to tell anything, not to repeat things already known, but so that hands far apart touch each other by touching the same sheet of paper. Barthes cites these words of Goethe:

Why do I see myself once gain compelled to write? It isn't necessary, my dear, to ask such an obvious questions because, in truth, I have nothing to tell you. However, your hands will receive this paper...

I return to Álvaro de Campos. Could this be the cause of the ridiculousness of love letters—the mismatch between what they say and that which they really want to do? Because the explicit purpose of a letter is to give news, and that's why they are made up of words. But what they really mean to accomplish is always above and beyond the written word. They want to accomplish that which separation prevents—a hug. Anyone who wants to try to understand a love letter through an analysis of the writing will always be off the mark because what it contains is that which isn't there, that which is absent. With any love letter, what matters isn't what's found written in it, only talk of desire, of the pain of absence, the longing to meet again.

That letter made everything stop. The woman closed the door and walked through the house without seeing anything, just looking for one thing, light, a place where the words would be illuminated. What difference does a chair make to her? She forgot that she's pregnant. Her eyes go over the words that came from the same hands that had hugged her. Her body is suspended in that magic moment of impossible affection that that little piece of paper opened in the time of her daily life.

A love letter is a paper that connects two lonelinesses. The woman is alone. If there are other people in the house, she's left them behind. It could very well be that the things written in the letter are no secret, that they can be told to everyone. But for it to be a love letter, it has to be read in solitude. As if the lover were saying, "I write so that you can be alone…" It is this act of solitary reading that establishes complicity. Because it was in loneliness that the letter was born. The love letter is an object the lover creates so the abandonment is tolerable.

I look at the sky. I see Alpha Centauri. The astronomers tell me that the star I see now is that star that was two years ago. Because that's the time that the light took to get to my eyes. What I see is that which no longer exists. And it would be useless for me to ask myself, "How is it now? Does it still exist?" I can get answers to these questions only two years from now, when its light reaches me. Its light is always late. I always see that which has already been... In this way letters are like stars. The letter that the woman has in her hands, which defines her moment of solitude, belongs to a moment that no longer exists. It says nothing about the present of the distant lover. Thus her pain. The lover who writes extends his arms to a moment that does not yet exist. The lover who reads extends her arms to a moment that no longer exists. The love letter is an embrace of space...

"It's good the phone exists," retort modern lovers who no longer have to live love in the space of absences. Mistake. A telephone call isn't a spoken letter because it lacks the essential. The silence of solitude, the calm of the pen poised over the table, waiting for and choosing thoughts and words. The telephone does away with solitude. In a telephone call we never say that which we would say in a letter. For example: "I was walking down the street when all of a sudden I saw a blossoming pink *ipê* tree that made me remember that time when...." Or "Re-reading Neruda's poems I found this one which I imagine you would like to read...."

The difference between a letter and a telephone is simple. The telephone is an imposition. The conversation

149

has to happen right then. It lacks the essential element of the word that is said without expecting a response. And once it's over, the two lovers are left with empty hands.

But the woman has in her hands a letter. The letter is an object. If she had not been able to take it into her solitude, she would have been able to put it away in her pocket in the delicious expectancy of an opportune moment. A telephone call can't wait. The letter is patient. It stores its words. And after being read, it can be re-read. Or simply caressed. A letter against the face—could anything be as loving? A letter is more than a message. Even before being read, even inside its closed envelope, it has the quality of a sacrament: a palpable presence of invisible happiness...

These thoughts came to me after reading the letters of a young scientist, Albert Einstein, to his girlfriend, Mileva Maric. It was they that led me to the poem by Álvaro de Campos. They were ridiculous. All love letters are ridiculous. I think the editors thought the same. And as an excuse for their indiscreet act of making public something ridiculous that was a secret between two lovers, they wrote a long and erudite introduction that transformed the ludicrous love letters into documents of the history of science. They were worth something because, mixed in with the ridiculousness the lovers fed each other the editors found trails that give historians keys for the understanding of "the sources of the emotional and intellectual development of the correspondents." Not knowing what to do with (ridiculous) love, they put the letters into the archeology of science.

It was then that Vermeer's painting had me see the scene that letters hide. And the woman with a letter in her hand and a child in her womb? She might very well be Mileva, pregnant with an illegitimate daughter that was given up for adoption and about whom nothing is known. The child was given up. But the letters were kept. And for what reasons might a person have to keep ridiculous letters? Her absorbed face and half-open lips give us an answer. For those who love, ridiculous love letters are always sublime. I return to Álvaro de Campos's poem and therein find what was needed to finish the scene: "but in the end, the only ridiculous things are creatures who have never written love letters."

Tennis and Matkot

After much meditation on the topic, I have concluded that there are two kinds of marriage. There are those of the tennis type and those of the matkot type.[12] Marriages of the tennis type are a source of anger and resentment, and they always end badly. Marriages of the matkot type are a source of joy and have a chance at a long life.

Let me explain. To begin, an affirmation from Nietzsche, with whom I agree entirely. He said that, on thinking about the possibility of marriage, everyone should ask themselves this question: "Do you believe you will be capable of conversing with this person into old age?" Everything else in marriage is transitory, but the relations that challenge time are those built around the art of

---

12   Matkot is a popular beach game resembling beach tennis. It typically involves two or more people hitting a rubber ball back and forth with rackets, the object being to extend the volley as long as possible.

conversation.

Scheherazade knew this. She knew that marriages based on the pleasures of the bed are always decapitated come morning, they end in separation because the pleasures of sex rapidly drain themselves and end in death, like in the Ogisa Noshima film *In the Realm of the Senses*. For that reason, when sex is dead in bed and love can no longer be spoken for through it, Scheherazade resuscitated it through the magic of the word. She started a long conversation, talk without end that would have to last a thousand and one nights. The sultan hushed and listened to her words as if they were music. The music of sounds or of words—it's sexuality in the form of eternity. It's love that always resuscitates after dying. There are caresses done with the body, and there are caresses done with words. And contrary to what inexperienced lovers think, caressing with words isn't all the time repeating "I love you, I love you..." Barthes warns: "Once that first confession has passed, 'I love you' doesn't say anything." And in talking, our true body shows itself not in anatomical nakedness but in poetic nakedness. Remember the wisdom of Adélia Prado: "The erotic is in the soul."

Tennis is a ferocious game. It's object is to defeat the adversary. And the adversary's defeat is revealed in his or her error: The opponent is incapable of returning the ball. Tennis is played to make the other err. The good player is the one who has the exact notion of her opponent's weak point, and it is exactly there that she tries to drive home her slice—a very suggestive word that indicates the sadistic objective, which is to slice, cut off, defeat. The pleasure of tennis is found, therefore, exactly at the moment in which the game can no longer go on because the adversary has been put out of play. It always ends with the happiness of one and the sadness of the other.

Matkot looks a lot like tennis: two players, two rackets, and a ball. But for the game to be good, neither of the two must lose. If the ball comes in a little out of line, the players know that it wasn't on purpose and make the greatest effort in the world to return it nicely, in the right place, so that the other person can get it. There's no adversary because there's no one to defeat. Here either the two win or nobody wins. And nobody becomes happy when the other errs—because the desire is that no one err. The error of one, in matkot, is like premature ejaculation: an unfortunate accident that shouldn't have happened since the pleasure is that back-and-forth, back-and-forth, back-and-forth... And the one who errs asks to be forgiven, and the one who caused the error feels blame. But it doesn't matter. The delightful game in which no one keeps score starts up again.

The ball. Iit's our fantasies, unrealities, dreams in the form of words. To converse is to be hitting a dream over

154

here, a dream over there...

But there are couples who play with dreams as if playing tennis. They wait for the right moment for the slice. Camus noted in his diary of small fragments for books he intended to write. One of them, found in *Notebooks 1935-1945*, is about this game of tennis:

> Scene: a husband, a wife, a choir. The first is worth something and likes to shine. The second keeps her silence, but, with short, dry sentences, she destroys all the propositions of her dear husband. In this way she constantly establishes her superiority. The other dominates but suffers humiliation, and from that, hatred is born. Example: with a small, "don't be dumber than you already are, my friend." The choir cheers and chuckles at will. He blushes, comes to her, kisses her hand, whispering, "You're right, my dear." The situation is saved and the hatred builds.

Tennis is like that: The other person's dream is received so that it can be destroyed, burst like a soap bubble. What is sought is to be right, and what is won is a distancing. Here, whoever wins loses.

In matkot, it's different. The dream of the other person is a game that must be kept going because it is understood that, if it's a dream, its a delight from the heart.

The good listener is that one who, when speaking, opens spaces where the soap bubbles can fly free. The ball goes back and forth...and love grows. No one wins so that they both can win. And so they wish that the other might live forever, eternally, so the game is never over.

"And the old shall fall in love anew..."

My friend didn't arrive at the set time. He called me to tell me he was at a wake. He arrived late, smiling. And he told me that outside the wake that happiness had come to him. I thought that the deceased must have been an enemy. It wasn't. An uncle, very dear to him, a sweet guy, 82 years old. And he told me a love story. As he spoke, my thoughts jumped around. First, I remembered the love of Florentino Ariza and Firmina Daza. Then, it was the love of T.S. Eliot and Valerie. All of them were loves in old age.

Young love is beautiful, but it isn't shocking. The young just have to fall in love. Romeo and Juliet is the one everybody considers normal. But love in old age is a shock because it reveals that the heart never ages. It can even

157

die, but it dies young. "Requited love always rejuvenates," Eliot said in the vigor of his passion, at the age of 70...

It's there in *Love in a Time of Cholera*, by Gabriel García Marquez. Anyone who hasn't read it is missing a unique experience in happiness...It was Florentino Ariza, a boy, who fell in love with Firmina Daza, an adolescent— crazy, crazy love, and only from a distance. The girl was closely watched. Notes and professions of love were exchanged in hidden places, all in the promise of the pleasure of someday an embrace. But in the time of cholera, things were different, and Firmina's father arranged a marriage with Dr. Urbino, an illustrious and prosperous medical doctor from town. Poor Florentino, lashed by futile love, from then on living in the insane hope that one day, never mind when, Firmina would be his. It was a wait of 51 years before the miracle happened. Dr. Urbino, unaware that time had passed, got up on an unsteady chair to rescue a parrot that had flown from the cage, and he set himself on a branch of a mango tree. The fall was unexpected and fatal. All of a sudden Dr. Urbano was plunked on the ground, neck broken. Once the period of mourning was over, the most beautiful love story of two old people began, love of sight and word, delight in the eyes, delight in the body.

I know very well that it was weird. Simone de Beauvoir, in her book on old age, says that there is something that is not lost in the elderly: that they can love with the same love as kids. Another kind of love is reserved for the old, a love for grandchildren, always patiently smiling, a resigned look, waiting for death, slow walks through the parks, hours spent playing patience, naps in the middle of conversations. But when the old resuscitate, and in their bodies the dormant powers of love rise again—oh! the kids are horrified! "He's gone senile!"

The story that my friend told me seemed like that of Florentino and Firmina. Only that the wait was much longer. Adolescent love interrupted—each one of them following his or her path, different, other loves, other families. But time didn't manage to turn it off. Psychoanalysts believe that time does not exist in the unconscious. We are eternally young. And, all of a sudden, already in the twilight, trees everyone figures are dried up begin to sprout and flower. They get married—he at 80, she 76—and they're going to live far away, far from the eyes of those who can't stand love in old age. And he, at 81, went back to study violin! Divine insanity! And he relearned the old words of love and said, as a realist, that if God let him live with her for just two years, he would be very happy. He didn't get two. He got one... And I got to thinking that year must have been like those rare experiences people have, and that cause to sprout, deep in the soul, that cry of exaltation à la Zorba, "It was worth the universe being created just for this!"

And it was the same that happened to T.S. Eliot, who

found his love only at 68, and at 70 said, before getting married, that he had been getting old. But now he felt younger than he had when he was 60.

Love has that magical capacity to make time run backwards. It isn't time that causes age, it's routine, vapidity, the incapacity to be moved by the smile of a woman or a man. But could it really be incapacity? Or could it be something else—that all of society has taught the elderly that the time for love has passed, that the price of being loved by your children and grandchildren is the renunciation of your dreams of love?

I understood my friend's happiness. And I became happy, too. That wake was a reminderl that comes at the end of a sonata, the culmination of happiness. It's interesting that, as a rule, the final movement of sonatas is an allegro. The adagios lamentosos are left behind. The conclusion ought to be an orgasm of joy. And, if I may, it should be appended to the sacred texts, in the places where the prophets have visions of messianic happiness, this other vision that, I believe, even God Himself would approve of with a smile: "And the old shall fall in love anew..."

It's in Talking that We Misunderstand

It's early morning, that confusing interlude between being asleep and awake, that the gods give me their revelations. So it happens that the more banal things appear before me from behind, which takes me by surprise because, from behind, things are the opposite of what they seem to be from the front.

Today, for example, the gods revealed to me that separation comes from understanding. For us to be together, it's best not to understand. This is the opposite of what couples think when they live in constant argument. They think their fights are because they don't understand each other, so they ask therapists for help, because who knows, maybe the therapist will help them understand each other better, which is a fact, but the conclusion doesn't follow from the premise. It isn't certain that after they understand each other they'll remain together.

Often it's at the precise moment of understanding that separation becomes inevitable. Nothing guarantees that understanding will be nice. The proof of this is what happened to my father-in-law, who hated brain. Invited to a dinner, he tasted a wonderful breaded cauliflower, enjoyed it, helped himself to seconds, and filled himself right up with it. After the meal, he complimented the hostess on the divine dish. But then she explained: "It isn't cauliflower, it's breaded brain..." —and he understood. And the understanding catapulted him in the direction of the nearest bathroom, where he heaved up the meal. That's how it is. Sometimes, when people don't understand something, they eat and enjoy. When they understand, the get disgusted and vomit.

Backwards statements like that, so contrary to common sense, demand an explanation—and that's what I'm coming around to do by means of a long curve which, in non-Euclidean geometry, is the shortest distant between two points.

162

In my computer I opened a file with the name "Encyclicals." There I put the text of encyclicals that I will promulgate when I am elected pope. As you know. Pope Leo XIII, in 1891, promulgated the encyclical *De Rerum Novarium*, which means "On New Things." All of a sudden, the church, which until then believed that everything worth knowing was stored in its millennial chest of doctrines, understood, with fright, that extremely new and interesting things were happening in the world.

And the good pope hurried to pass this information on. This was the beginning of an enormous modernization effort by the church that didn't work out because you don't put a patch of new cloth on old cloth. The old cloth had just started to tear... Wishing to repair the bad the *De Rerum Novarum* had caused, I wrote its antithesis, the encyclical *De Rerum Vetustarum*, or "On Old Things."

And its substance is extraordinarily simple. The encyclical prays that, from the moment of its publication, everything, absolutely everything that happens in the Church, the liturgies, the priestly blessings, the baptisms, the christenings, weddings, funerals, hymns, readings of the Holy scripture, sermons, encyclicals, and even the words of the father in the confessional, everything would have to be done in Latin. Ah! How beautiful Latin is! It sounds like a "liturgy of crystal," pure music.

Music is poetry at its highest point, when the words completely lose any meaning and transform into pure beauty, beauty that doesn't look for meanings. Ineffable beauty without words. There can be no squabbles over music. So, if everything in the Church happened in Latin, it would be as if it were only music—there would be no

163

possibility of misunderstandings.

If the priests and the bishops spoke in Latin, we wouldn't understand anything, and we would love everything. Because music is like that. We love it without understanding it. The Oracle of Delphi, wise and smart, knew that quite well and never said anything that others understood. Clear, distinct language kills fantasy. She spoke her enigmas, pure music, in strange language. It isn't by chance that the Pentecostals and Charismatics grow the way they do: by the power of a strange language that no one understands. Everything fits inside that which no one understands. Brain turns to cauliflower, and the body and mind approve.

I would really like to visit a monastery where speaking prose is prohibited—where only poetry is read and stories told—and music is heard, Gregorian chants, Bach, the saxophone of Jan Garbarek, the piano of Keith Jarrett, the Carmina Burana, Jean-Pierre Rampal playing Japanese melodies, Maurice André and his trumpet... Or a Quaker congregation where silence is nurtured, no one speaks, everyone listens, the voice of God heard only when everyone is quiet.

Understanding always causes fights. I really imagine that that's why God confused the language of humanity in the construction of the Tower of Babel. People spoke the same language. Speaking, they understood each other.

Understanding each other, they understood each others' opinions. Understanding each others' opinions, they didn't like each other. Then came the fights. God All-Powerful then understood that the only way to avoid fighting was to make it so they couldn't understand each other. And thus was born music, the language that no one understands and everyone loves.

It's in talking that we misunderstand each other. At some future moment, I will continue my torturous wanderings, passing the church, the place where eternal marriages are blessed, to arrive at home, place where we know that marriages are ephemeral. For now, I stick with my advice for couples who are fighting. Be careful with talk. From talk understanding can be born, from understanding separation can happen. Understanding can be as fatal for marriage as it was for my father-in-law's dinner. It's in talk that we misunderstand each other.

Avoid marriage counseling. It can lead to intolerable understanding. Understanding can lead to insanity. There are insanities that can result from clarity of thought... Adopt the millennial wisdom of the Church. Adopt Latin as the language of your house. And dedicate yourselves to music, with preference for wind instruments, because while you're blowing in them, you can't talk and thus understanding and separations are avoided.

165

For a Wedding

Love is given for free,
sown in the wind, in the waterfall,
in the eclipse...
Carlos Drummond de Andrade

My fascination with rites makes me suspect that in another life I may have been a priest or sorcerer. Today, few people know what they are. A rite takes place when a poem, believing that words are not enough, manifests itself in acts, in food and drink, in colors and aromas, in music and dance. The rite is a poem transformed into a party! Today I write for those who marry. I fear that, fascinated by a rite, they forget one another... Because in case they don't know it, it's that other person, forgotten, that the marriage depends on.

The first rite, which everybody knows about and for which invitations are made, is done with rocks, iron, and cement.

There's another rite, a secret one, that is carried out with the flight of birds, with water, breeze, foam, and soap bubbles.

The first rite was born of a mixture of joy and sadness. Seeing the flight of birds, they felt happy. But then the birds were gone, and they became sad. It wasn't enough that the happiness was infinite while it lasted. They wanted it to be eternal. And they said: "We want the flight of birds eternally." And what better thing is there for containing the flight of birds than a cage? So that's what they did. They caged the bird and called in the sorcerers, ordering them to speak the words of sorcery: "Forever, until death do we part."

The most precise definition of this rite I heard from the mouth of a priest: "It isn't love that makes a marriage," he affirmed. "It's the vows."

I was shocked. I knew it was like that in civil marriage contracts, society's cold rite defining the obligations (on the pleasures it is silent) and the sharing of the better and worse. Society is a solid thing. It needs stone, iron, and cement. Guarantees. Witnesses. Documents. The future is supposed to be the way the present planned it. For that, we have contracts. And the substance of a contract is the vows. Yes. He was right. "It isn't the love that makes a marriage. It's the vows."

Vows are words that encage the future. That's why

they are always done with witnesses. If the caged bird, at some moment in the future, changes its feelings and its mind and decides to fly away, the witnesses are there to affirm the vows made in the past. The spoken and contracted cannot be changed.

Many are the vows that bride and groom can take: I promise to divide all my goods, I promise to not treat her badly, I promise not to humiliate him, I promise to protect her, I promise to take care of you in sickness. Exterior acts can be promised.

That's how marriages are made, with stone, iron, cement, and love. But the stuff of love cannot be promised. I can't promise that, for the rest of my life, I will smile with joy when I hear your name. I can't promise that, for the rest of my life, I will miss you when you're away.

Feelings can't be promised. They can't be promised because they don't depend on our will. Their existence is ephemeral. They only exist in the moment. Like the flight of birds, the blowing of the wind, the colors at twilight. This is a rite of adults because only adults wish that the future might be the same as the present. Its weight, its seriousness, its cadenced and processional footsteps, its clothes, its masks, the sacred words, definitive, forever, what God brings together man cannot separate, the exaltation of obligations. Everything testifies that this is a ritual of adults.

The other ritual is done with the flight of birds, with

168

water, foam, and soap bubbles. It's secret. There are no invitations. The marriage of Abelard and Heloise, the most beautiful love ever lived (prohibited) was secret.

There are no invitations, no certain place, no set time. It just happens. "Love is given for free / sown in the wind / in the waterfall / in the eclipse..." (Drummond). There's no need for altars: Whenever it happens, a rainbow appears: God's vow, because God is love. It could be the shade of a tree, a car, a kitchen, a garden bench, the coach of a train, an airport, a table in a bar, a walk in moonlight...

No vows tie down the future. There are professions of love to celebrate the present. "How you are precious, my love, how you are precious! There is honey under your tongue!" "Your cheek, my love, is balsam and your lips are lilies." (*Holy Bible*) "I know that I will love you / for my whole life I will love you / with every good-bye I will love you / desperately I know that I will love you..." (Vinicius de Morães); "I love you, man, I love your heart, what it is, the flesh of which it is made, I love your material, fauna and flower (...) I love you with memory imperishable." (Adélia Prado)

And the invitees, the very few, dress like children— bare feet, colorful balloons in their hands. They know that love remains only if we remain children eternally...

Ego conjugo vobis in matrimonium, says the old man with the face of a child.

For you I invoke the pleasures that fly in the winds and the joys that reside in colors, beauty, harmony, enchantment, magic, mystery, poetry. May these divine powers keep you company.

May the smile of one be, for the other, a festival, a banquet, honey, fish roasted on the fire, ripe coconut on the beach, salty wave of the sea...

May the words of the other be white cloth, a transparent dress of joy to be unclothed by subtle charm.

And may, in the end and in the beginning, in the name of the name unsaid, well said, in the name of all the absent and nostalgic names present here, of *agapé* and *philos*, friendship and love, in the name of the holy name, of the broken bread and drunken wine, may the two be happy, today, tomorrow, and always...

Auditory

I always see ads for courses in oratory—the art of speaking. I've never seen an ad for a course in auditory—the art of listening. Everybody wants to learn to speak. I've thought about offering a course in auditory. But I don't think anyone will enroll.

Listening is complicated and subtle. Alberto Caeiro said, "It isn't enough to not be blind to trees and flowers. You also need to not have any philosophy whatsoever." Philosophy is a pile of ideas—inside the head, about how things are. So we who are not blind open our eyes. Before us, outside the head, in the fields and forests, are the trees and flowers. To see is to put inside the head that which exists outside the head. The blind don't see because their windows are closed. What is outside doesn't manage to enter. We aren't blind. The trees and flowers get in. But—

poor things—they come in and fall into a sea of ideas. They are mixed into the words of philosophy that live within us. They lose their simplicity of existence. They become other things. Therefore, what we see isn't trees and flowers. For them to be seen, the head must be empty.

It's been a long time, but I've never forgotten. I was going by bus. Behind me, two women were talking. One of them told her friend about her suffering. (A friend from the harsh and impoverished northeast of Brazil, told me that women from the Northeast like to play a game when they talk with each other. They compare each other's suffering. The greater the suffering, the more beautiful the women and their lives. Conversation is the art of putting one's self forward as a woman of suffering. I think that that's where opera was invented. The soul is a literature. It is on this that psychoanalysis is based…) Getting back to the bus. They were taking about suffering. One of them talked about her husband in the hospital, the doctors, the complicated exams, the injections in the vein—the nurse never hit it right—the vomit and the urine. It was a moving tale of pain. Until the tale came to the end, expecting, apparently applause, admiration, a word of sheltering in the soul of the other, who was, supposedly, listening. But what the suffering one heard was: "But that's nothing…." The other woman then began a story of suffering incomparably more terrible, something worthy of an opera of first-rate suffering.

Rubem Alves

Let me paraphrase Albert Camus: "It isn't enough to have ears to hear what's said. You also need to have silence in your soul." From that, a difficulty: we can't stand to hear what the other says without offering an opinion that's a little better, without mixing that which he said with that which we have to say. As if that which he said weren't worth thoughtful consideration and needed to be complemented by that which we had to say, which is much better. Down deep we are just like the women on the bus. Lichtenberg was right—as cited by Murilo Mendes: "There are people who won't hear until their ears are cut off." Our incapacity to hear is the most constant and subtle manifestation of our arrogance and vanity. Down deep, we are the most beautiful...

I have an old friend, Jovelino, who moved to the United States, motivated by the 1964 military revolution. He was a Protestant minister (not "evangelical"). He went to work in an educational program of the Presbyterian Church, aimed at minorities. He told me about this experience with the Indians. The meetings were strange. When everybody got together, nobody talked. There was a long, long silence. (Pianists, before starting a concert, will sit in silence before the piano as if they were communing. Not praying. Communing. Opening space in the silence. Expelling all outside ideas. Playing piano, too, requires that one have no philosophy whatsoever.) Everyone in silence, awaiting the essential thought. Then all of a sudden someone speaks. It's short. Everyone listens. When the speaking's done, new silence. To speak right away would be a disrespect since the other person had spoken his or her thoughts, thoughts that he or she judged to be essential. Being of someone else, the thoughts are not mine. They are foreign to me. Food to be digested. Digestion takes time. You need time to understand what the other said.

If I speak right away, there are two possibilities.

First: "I remained silent only to be polite. In truth, I didn't hear what you said. While you were speaking, I was thinking about the things I was going to say when you finished your (foolish) speech. I speak as if you hadn't spoken."

Second: "I heard what you said. But what you said as something new I'd already thought a long time ago. For me, it's something old. So old that I don't even need to think about what you said."

In both cases, I'm calling the other person a fool. Which is worse than a slap in the face. The long silence means to say, "I am carefully pondering everything you said." And so goes the meeting.

There are religious groups whose liturgy consists of silence. Some years ago I spent a week in a monastery in Switzerland. Grands Champs. Some other people and I

174

were there, together, to write a book. It was an old farm. Old buildings. I can't forget the water from the fountain where the pigeons came to drink. The silence was disciplined, not total, but of minimum talk. Which gave me enormous pleasure at meals. There was no need to maintain a conversation with my table mates. I could eat while thinking about the food. Eating also requires one to have no philosophy. To not have an obligation to speak is a pleasure. But then I was informed that part of the discipline at the monastery was to take part in the liturgy three times a day: at seven in the morning, at noon, and at six in the evening. I shook with fear. But I obeyed. The sacred space was an old barn, all wood, a high ceiling. Dark. There were open holes in the wood with glass of various colors set in them. It was an atmosphere of dim light lit by a few candles on the altar, a simple table with an oriental icon of Christ. A few pews arranged in a U-shape set off an ample empty space in the center where whoever wanted to could sit on a pillow on a carpet. I arrived a few minutes before the set time. It was a grand silence. It was cold. Dark clouds covered the sky and rushed by, carried by an impetuous wind that descended from the Alps. The force of the wind was so great that the old barn twisted and creaked as if it were a wooden ship on rough seas. The wind beat on the naked apple trees in the orchard, and the sound was like breaking waves. I found it strange. The Swiss are always punctual. The liturgy wasn't starting. No one was getting things underway. Everybody went on like that, without doing anything. No one got up to say, "My brothers, let us sing a hymn…" Five minutes, ten, fifteen. Only after twenty minutes did I, idiot, notice that everything had started twenty minutes ago. people were there to feed on the silence. And I, too, began to feed on the silence. Silence on the outside isn't enough. You need silence inside. An absence of thought. And then, when you've made silence on the inside, you begin to hear things you'd never heard. I began to hear.

Fernando Pessoa knew the experience and referred to something that is heard in the interstices of words, in the place where there are no words. It's music, melody that wasn't there before and which, once heard, makes us weep. Music happens in silence. The noises have to stop. In silence, doors open to an enchanted world that lives inside us—as in Malarmé's poem "The Submerged Cathedral," which Debussy put to music. The soul is a submerged cathedral. In the bottom of the sea—anyone who dives knows—the mouth stays shut. We're all eyes and ears. Just now the idea came to me that maybe this is the essence of the religious experience—when we become mute, without speaking. Then, free of the noise of the talkatory and the wisdoms of philosophy, we hear the melody that wasn't

176

there, so beautiful it makes us weep. Hence the importance of knowing how to listen to others. Beauty lives there, too. Communion is when the other's beauty and our beauty come together in counterpoint.

Acknowledgements

This translation was made possible with the intellectual support of Raquel Alves and the Instituto Rubem Alves, senior translation editor Ana Lessa-Schmidt, who also wrote the Introduction. New London Librarium senior editors Ralph Cheney and Denise Dembinski applied their critical eyes to the text.

About Rubem Alves

Rubem Alves (1933—2014) was a theologian, philosopher, educator, psychoanalyst, and one of Brazil's most popular writers. Born in Boa Esperança, Minas Gerais, he went on to earn a Ph.D. from Princeton Theological Seminary. He also trained and practiced as a psychoanalyst. His most recent professorship was at the Universidade Estadual at Campinas. He is the author of hundreds of essays and 40 books on pedagogy, theology, philosophy, and life in general. His works have been published in 13 countries and translated into various languages. More information is available at the Instituto Rubem Alves in Campinas, São Paulo State, Brazil (www.rubemalves.com.br).

About Raquel Alves

Raquel Nopper Alves is the youngest of three children of Rubem Alves. With her birth, his view of the world changed. He began to write only that which would come from his heart.

Raquel earned an undergraduate degree in landscape architecture and urbanism and Master's degree in Urbanism before working 15 years as a landscape architect. And just as her birth transformed the life of the writer, the death of her father in 2014 transformed her, too. She carries within her the fruit of seeds he nurtured. For that reason, she gave up landscape architecture and became director and president of the Instituto Rubem Alves, which was founded to disseminate and eternalize the work and legacy of the writer.

About the Translator

Glenn Alan Cheney is a translator, writer, and editor in Hanover, Conn. His more than 25 books explore myriad topics, including Brazil, nuns, Chernobyl, nuclear issues, the Pilgrims, Abraham Lincoln, bees, and Swaziland, as well as novels, stories, poems, and essays. He is the founder and managing editor of New London Librarium.

Lightning Source UK Ltd.
Milton Keynes UK
UKHW010303190722
406028UK00003B/92/J